EVERYDAY
APOCALYPSE

EVERYDAY APOCALYPSE

The Sacred Revealed in Radiohead,
The Simpsons, *and Other Pop Culture Icons*

DAVID DARK

Brazos Press
A Division of Baker Book House Co
Grand Rapids, Michigan 49516

© 2002 by David Dark

Published by Brazos Press
a division of Baker Book House Company
P.O. Box 6287, Grand Rapids, MI 49516-6287

Printed in the United States of America

Scripture is taken from the New Revised Standard Version of the Bible, copyright 1989 by the Division of Christian Education of the National Council of the Churches of Christ in the USA. Used by permission.

Library of Congress Cataloging-in-Publication Data

Dark, David, 1969–
    Everyday Apocalypse : the sacred revealed in Radiohead, the Simpsons, and other pop culture icons / David Dark.
        p.   cm.
    Includes bibliographical references.
    ISBN 1-58743-055-X (pbk.)
    1. Popular culture—Religious aspects—Christianity. 2. Christianity and culture. 3. Mass media—Religious aspects—Christianity. 4. Apocalyptic literature—History and criticism. I. Title.
BR115.C8 D37 2002
261—dc21   2002011702

For current information about all releases from Brazos Press, visit our web site:
http://www.brazospress.com

Dedication:
To Sarah
Who emanates apocalyptic

Contents

Acknowledgments:

Crucial encouragement in the direction of the present work came early on through the generosity of Steve and Janice Stockman, Dwight Ozard, Charlie Peacock, Jay Swartzendruber, Douglas Kaine McKelvey, Nick Barre, Shelley Stephens, Melissa Palladino, John Wilson of *Books and Culture,* and Steve Taylor. I've also been sustained by long-term votes of confidence from Michael and Cary Blythman, Dave and Ollie Adams, Ewan Gibson, Chris Fry, Jude Adam, Jenna Galbreth, Trevor Henderson, Mark McCleary, and Gareth Higgins. Anything clever or illuminating in my writing probably originates from fellowship and conversational tangents sponsored by the likes of Todd and Rusti Greene (Psalm 139 and "instant nostalgia"), Lee and Judith Smithey, Melinda Franklin, Liz Toohey, Geoff Little, Lon Bouldin, Randall Lancaster, Tom Wills, Andy Harding, Julie Lee, Gar and Autumn Saegar, and Wade Jaynes. Thanks are also due to Dave and Sue Perkins, Michael and Marilyn Wilson, Rob and Alexia Bancroft, Bill and Brenda Mallonnee, and James Stewart. For ongoing support in the classroom, I'm deeply indebted to Mitch and Kara Menning, Phil Boeing, Joy MacKenzie, and Terri Eaves. And for patience and a willingness to at least maintain the appearance of interest, I'd like to thank my families: the Darks, Masens, Sharps, Lovetts, Foremans, and Wileys. Personal invigoration has been derived from the artistic determination of the Anthropic Collective, the solidarity of the Ekklesia Project, the indispensable work of Christian Aid, and the intelligently designed music of Michael Sandison and Marcus Eoin of Boards of Canada. Finally, my gratitude goes out to Rodney Clapp and Rebecca Cooper, whose editing and fine-tuning have gone a long way in keeping me from embarrassing myself.

ONE

Flip the Script

Apocalyptic and the Lyricism of Protest

Art's necessary illusions serve to expose the illusory character of the experienced world. . . . Artists of necessity refer to the given world, yet to be art their work must imply (refer to) a whole new world of unrealized possibility.

James William McClendon
Witness: Systematic Theology, volume III

As a literary genre, "apocalyptic" is a way of investing space-time events with their theological significance; it is actually a way of affirming, not denying, the vital importance of the present continuing space-time order, by denying that evil has the last word in it.

N. T. Wright
The New Testament and the People of God

We apparently have the word "apocalypse" all wrong. In its root meaning, it's not about destruction or fortune-telling; it's about revealing. It's what James Joyce calls an epiphany—the moment you realize that all your so-called love for the young lady, all your professions, all your dreams, and all your efforts to get her to notice you were the exercise of an unkind and obsessive vanity. It wasn't about her at all. It was all about you. The real world, within which you've lived and moved and had your being, has unveiled itself. It's starting to come to you. You aren't who you made yourself out to be. An apocalypse has just occurred, or a revelation, if you prefer.

Apocalyptic changes everything. Its intense attentiveness to the minute particulars, to the infinity forever passing before our eyes, can leave us feeling ashamed of our ongoing impenetrability to the immediate. It creates an unrest within our minds, and it can only be overcome by imagining differently, by giving in to its aesthetic authority, by letting it invigorate the lazy conscience.

Apocalyptic shows us what we're not seeing. It can't be composed or spoken by the powers that be, because they are the sustainers of "the way things are" whose operation justifies itself by crowning itself as "the way things ought to be" and whose greatest virtue is in being "realistic." Thinking through what we mean when we say "realistic" is where apocalyptic begins. If these powers are the boot that, to borrow Orwell's phrase, presses down upon the human face forever, apocalyptic is the speech of that human face. Apocalyptic denies, in spite of all the appearances to the contrary, the "forever" part.

For both the very human wielder of the boot and the very human face beneath it, apocalyptic has a way of curing deafness and educating the mind. In our confusion, we're accustomed to according the titles of good news and "a positive message" to the most soul-sucking, sentimental fare imaginable. Any song or story that deals with conflict by way of a strained euphemistic spin, a cliche, or a triumphal cupcake ending strikes us as the best in family entertainment. This is the opposite of apocalyptic. Apocalyptic maximizes the reality of human suffering and folly before daring a word of hope (lest too light winning make the prize light). The hope has nowhere else to happen but the valley of the shadow of death. Is it any surprise that we often won't know it when we see it?

10

Goodbye Cruel World

Our ability to recognize apocalyptic is, in our day, often most hindered by the popular, best-selling misunderstandings of biblical witness. Confusing the death-dealing forces that enslave, exploit, and crucify (what our biblical translations sometimes render "the world") for the created world itself, such so-called "apocalyptic" is a negation of this-worldly experience. It tends to view the physical as only fit for burning. In a kind of Gnostic-style propaganda, creation is deemed a sort of waiting room, irredeemable and best discarded. Confusing redemption for escape, real injustice—political and personal—goes mostly unengaged, and the actual, everyday world gets left behind.

In this view, apocalyptic is simply equated with disaster or destruction, and the biblical summons to full-bodied, incarnate witness against dehumanization is exchanged for an almost nihilistic contempt for anything down-to-earth or, in the most meaningful sense, human. The big revelation of orthodox faith is renounced for a big removal that can smugly disregard the immediately physical as spiritually irrelevant. The big redemption (already in progress) of biblical witness is transmogrified into a big annihilation peculiarly well-suited to a mostly unincarnate faith that is often more than willing to help the earth along toward its impending destruction. Against the announcement of a new day to come *on earth* as it is in heaven, this heretical worldview can avoid the political implications of the new day coming by confining it to a "spiritual issue," whatever that means.

But genuinely apocalyptic expression is a radical declaration concerning the meaning of human experience. Its job is to reflect, in a deeply liberating fashion, the tensions and paradoxes that constitute our understanding of reality. In lively contrast to any negation of creation, it actually accords our words, actions, and relationships an infinite importance by breaking down constructs of selfishness and self-delusion and challenging our concepts of power and profit. By announcing a new world of unrealized possibility, apocalyptic serves to invest the details of the everyday with cosmic significance while awakening its audience to the presence of marginalizing forces otherwise unnamed and unchallenged.

Through bold acts of the imagination, apocalyptic presents itself to its audience in a manner unmoved by the names of kings and presidents and corporations but very much moved by a realm beyond their sceptered sway. This realm, incidentally, will not be confined to an antiquated past, to some culturally captivated present, or to some future era that begins with people disappearing from airplanes. Instead, apocalyptic offers a world that is and was and is to come, a world spinning inside (and outside) this one. Unlike the "realistic" world of boot-on-face, "final solutions," and collateral damage, apocalyptic announces a world without end.

Apocalyptic cracks the pavement of the status quo. It irritates and disrupts the feverishly defended norms of whatever culture it engages. In the case of the American South of the early 1800s, for instance, the black leather-bound document with the family tree in the front and the stories, songs, letters, and laws in King James English appeared to buttress everything the slave-owning landholder viewed as good and right and true. But the language and imagery of the biblical tradition would embody a very different impression in the African-American church. The captor was beginning to look an awful lot like Egypt. The language of the prophets will accommodate (indeed, insist upon) a socially disruptive newness: "Behold, I will do a new thing; now it shall spring forth; shall ye not know it? I will even make a way in the wilderness, and rivers in the desert" (Isaiah 43:19). Surely this meant more than white people going to heaven. Greater apocalypses have ways of developing within the old, domesticated ones. When this happens, it literally makes history.

In this sense, apocalyptic is the place where the future pushes into the present. It's the breaking in of another dimension, a new wine for which our old wineskins are unprepared. That which apocalyptic proclaims cannot be fit into existing ways of thinking. Wynton Marsalis describes classical music as "harmony through harmony" and jazz as "harmony through conflict."[1] When we bring this way of putting the matter to the Bible, we find little in the way of classical music and plenty in the way of jazz, especially in the passages categorized as apocalyptic—whether it's trees clapping their hands, stars falling from the sky, bloody red moons, or crystal seas. It's as if the new world on the way requires constant rearticulation to best bear witness of its freshness and new-every-morningness, perpetually straining forward to what lies ahead. At its best, jazz itself (with origins not unrelated to the bold imagination of the African-American church) gives voice to the groaning universe anticipating a new day. This is the business of apocalyptic.

"Sir, you better take a look at this."

Given our tendency to see and hear what we want to see and hear while disregarding the rest, we need whatever we can get in the way of an awakening. The pictures and sounds and stories of apocalyptic expression are deliberately paradoxical in such a way that they tease the mind out of whatever old, self-justifying forms it has settled for. This is apparently what Flannery O'Connor refers to as "distortion": "I am interested in making up a good case for distortion, as I am coming to believe it is the only way to make people see."[2]

Such distortion creates a tension within the audience's imagination, and while dismissing the distortion as out of hand won't relieve the tension, yielding to it will. We can recall the carefully staged apocalypse the prophet Nathan prepared for King David by way of a story designed to sabotage his moral obliviousness. Having arranged the death of Uriah the Hittite to better accommodate and cover up his sexual relationship with Uriah's wife, Bathsheba, David tried to continue his life and career protectively ignorant of his deeply depraved behavior. Enter Nathan with the unwelcome, enlightening word that is, nevertheless, crucial for the health of the king and his kingdom. Nathan's story of a pitiless, rich man and his needless thievery of a poor man's lamb sets David's pulse pounding with anger until he realizes that Nathan is holding up a mirror to his own treatment of Uriah. Apocalyptic won't flatter or privilege the powerful or congratulate us for our sincere intentions, but it will illumine what is dark. It will passionately expose. It will make us see.

Suddenly the world and the role we've played within it is a different place. We're made to know what's going on in such a powerful way that all manner of things are made new. This, according to N. T. Wright, is how stories (especially Jesus' parables) have always worked: "They invite listeners into a new world, and encourage them to make that world their own, to see their ordinary world from now on through this lens, within this grid. The struggle to understand a parable is the struggle for a new world to be born."[3]

The imagery of this new world, which Jesus employs in various ways ("The kingdom of God is like . . . ") and which audiences, then and now, struggle to understand, is inherited from the imagination of Israel. Throughout early Jewish literature, the "Day of the Lord" is anticipated and articulated as a new order in which God will decisively turn the tables, overcome the oppressor (Egypt, Babylon, Rome), and mandate *shalom,* a state of absolute flourishing, of everything in its right place in all creation forever. This announcement obviously has numerous implications for the occupying powers, who habitually have a pretension or two in the direction of "forever," but in the meantime, it's a summons to whomever has an ear to live lives radically oriented toward the upcoming (and hereby declared) deliverance.

Apocalyptic, correctly understood, reminds us that the language of "the kingdom of God" isn't referring to some politically irrelevant eternity of otherworldly existence. To say that it is "at hand" or "near" is a directive to "repent" and enter into a new way of life that aligns itself with the purposes of *shalom.*

If we miss the political significance of the Lord's Prayer, for instance, we entirely miss its meaning as a call for apocalypse *now* that acknowledges, invites, and pledges allegiance to the age to come while forcefully renouncing the legitimacy of whatever lesser gods compete for our adoration ("*Thine* is the kingdom and the power and the glory").

We're assisted in our understanding of what's at stake in these matters when we note John Milbank's description of the crucifixion and, we might add, the persecution of the early church as "the rejection by the political-economic order of a completely new sort of social imagination."[4] Apocalyptic was and is the only language adequate to describe this new beginning while maintaining its practice as one of constant exodus. It keeps religion strange and ready to question the given "reality" of the day. Without apocalyptic, no questioning occurs and the biblical voice is easily edited (or censored) to the point that it appears to support whatever sentimental sap or suburban self-improvement program it's pasted upon. What should have been, for starters, good news for the poor and down-trodden is neatly packaged (and quoted out of context) to look good beside a basket full of puppies on a greeting card. A political-economic order has nothing to fear from a sentimental, fully "spiritualized" faith.

We indulge a historical deafness when we think of the Jewish and Christian movements as the uncritical endorsers of whatever societal structures currently hold the population captive. It was Augustine, after all, who described earthly kingdoms as large-scale criminal syndicates. Few could have predicted that biblical language would become so tied up in social hierarchies that religion would become the object of critique rather than the acknowledged source of the critique itself. Perhaps this says as much for the movement's powers of infiltration as it does for the uses to which the language can be put outside of its context.

If, in our day, religion is seen as a machine whose purpose is the forgetting of history and the ongoing neglect of the world outside, apocalyptic is the maddening corrective. It resists the appropriation of biblical language to achieve the ends of ideology and overturns our assumptions about success, power, and effectiveness. It mercifully breaks down the images we use to congratulate ourselves. Without it, we're desperately ill-equipped to perceive the meaning of what's passing before our eyes in our immediate environment and beyond.

When we bring our wits to bear upon apocalyptic expression, we find that it has a way of unmasking the fictions we inhabit by breaking down, among other things, our constructs of public and private, political and religious, natural and spiritual. It's annoyingly resistant to our short-sighted either/or propositions and refuses all abstract (and in the case of biblical apocalyptic, anachronistic) divisions such as sacred/secular. For the apocalyptic mind, there isn't a secular molecule in the universe, no matter outside the scope of its coming kingdom, no nook or cranny exempt from the redemption it announces. Neither Jesus

15

nor any Jewish prophet ever instructed his listeners to merely repent "spiritually."

Apocalyptic Applicability

By now, my preference for that which I've placed under the umbrella of apocalyptic should be obvious. To the best of my knowledge, I've remained faithful to the scholarly consensus concerning the definition of apocalyptic as a literary genre. I'm about to expand the sphere of the definition by noting the presence of a distinctly apocalyptic impulse in certain examples of literature and, for lack of a better term, popular culture. In the final chapter of this book, we'll spread the umbrella even further to describe apocalyptic as a distinctive way of looking at and being within the world. In the meantime, I should probably distinguish between interpretations involving applicability and the uncovering of hidden agendas.

In his efforts to overcome the popular misreading of his work on Middle-earth as a project in allegory, J. R. R. Tolkien expressed a distaste for the domineering quality of the allegorical while offering a helpful distinction: "I much prefer history, true or feigned, with its varied applicability to the thought and experience of readers. I think that many confuse 'applicability' with 'allegory'; but the one resides in the freedom of the reader, and the other in the purposed domination of the author."[5]

"Purposed domination" is a wonderfully illuminating phrase in Tolkien's explanation not only in regard to what he assures us he *isn't* doing in *The Lord of the Rings* but also concerning a mode of creative expression to which he feels an almost moral aversion. Purposed domination, we might say, is the method of propaganda. It leaves the audience with no room for "applicability," and the propagandist wouldn't have it any other way. The tightly controlled "message," after all, was the point in the first place, *not* the dignity of the reader or the story (if we can even call it a story). In thinking through Tolkien's alternative, creative ethic, we can note, for instance, the example of Gandalf ("I do not wish for mastery") and contrast his politics with the obsessive machinations of Saruman.

16

My recognition of the apocalyptic quality present in various instances of artistic expression is an acknowledgment of applicability. I'm not insisting, for example, that the writers and production team of *The Simpsons* have self-consciously set out to bombard the airwaves with their hidden moral agenda. Applicability is another matter. If we're incapable of recognizing the subversive, satiric insight of something like *The Simpsons,* our ability to apply ourselves to the joys of interpretation, or to view art well at all, has proven itself deficient.

One peculiarity of the present age is that, in some cases, our powers of application are so compromised that we're incapable of recognizing as morally edifying anything that doesn't advertise itself as such. The most glaring example of this confusion is found in the million-dollar industry of marketing under the title of "Christian." Given our current cultural climate, the media consumer does well to be wary of any product that has featured, foremost among its selling points, it's so-called Christianness. Buyers with a taste for propaganda (and who soon find themselves strangely disinterested in anything that isn't) will find, in that which most loudly advertises itself as Christian, much in the way of crude moralism and plenty in the way of slogans and cliches that encourage blissful disregard of the soon-to-be-destroyed world around them. Often promoting an unincarnate faith, this phenomenon has more in common with the aforementioned Gnosticism than what can be understood as orthodox belief. I'm personally convinced that such market-driven theology will be viewed, historically, with at least as much embarrassment as, say, the medieval sale of indulgences.

One unfortunate by-product of religion as a marketing tool is the "Christian" consumer who finds himself embroiled in the psychological nightmare of trying to be a good advertisement for God. As Kathleen Norris has pointed out, advertising language is, by definition, fundamentally dishonest, and the cognitive dissonance involved in putting on a brave face and learning to like (and act like) "Christian" products is not easily underestimated. Perhaps worst of all, the believer is deprived of his inheritance, within the Jewish and Christian traditions, of an apocalyptic worldview. It is, after all, useless if not applied to the actual world. But in stark contrast to the doctrines of redemption and incarnation, the hapless buyer, trapped in the maze of "religious" marketing, is trained to view the sweet old world as "secular," which is to say irrelevant to his horrendously sentimentalized, "religious" experience. To a great extent, the believer is taught to try to "give God the glory" by dwelling in a world (not unlike *The Truman Show*) that God never made.

Apocalyptic, in my view, is the orthodox alternative. In spite of the dangers of marketing categories, my exercise in apocalyptic applicability strives to be understood as Christian. When holding forth on various topics, my specific allegiances inevitably come poking through: "Are you a Christian or something?" To avoid the pain of being pigeonholed, I've found it helpful to respond with something along the lines of "Describe what you mean by the word, and I'll tell you if you're describing me." In an attempt at defiance of the malicious impatience of a sound-bite culture, this procedure can give birth to that treasure of treasures: a genuine conversation.

The movement called Christianity (of which I know myself to be a recipient while aspiring to be a practitioner) cannot be understood apart from the Jewish concept of *shalom*. The Christian gospel does not call people to give their mental assent to a certain list of correct propositions, nor does it provide its adherents with a password that will gain them disembodied bliss when they die and the pleasure of confidently awaiting their escape until then. *Shalom* is a way of being *in the world*. The Christian gospel invites us to partake in *shalom,* to embody *shalom,* and to anticipate its full realization in the coming kingdom of God.

Yes and No

In our everyday experience, any announcement of *shalom* will be both a Yes and a No. Yes, life is beautiful. When we look at the face of a human being, we're gazing upon a living mystery of infinite worth. We were made for something better than what we're getting and whatever it is we're settling for. This can't be all there is, which leads us into the No. Is the gated community the best of all possible words? No. Do we deserve our riches? Is the actor happy? Are we civilized? Power constellations: "Whatever is, is right." Apocalyptic: "No."

Apocalyptic shows culture that its claims about itself aren't true. It reprimands us for the ways in which we've hoped to manage life into a grid or pattern that can control the messiness. These grids spare us the tension of thought and imagination when confronted with the uncategorizability of the human being. In the company of our fellow uncategorizable humans and in the face of the cosmically holy everyday, such pride is evil, certainly, but apocalyptic will often satisfy itself, for the time being, with the insight that our grid-building tendencies are silly, foolish, and metaphysically unsound.

The present work concerns itself with all manner of media that highlights, exposes, or lampoons the moral bankruptcy of our imaginations while teasing us toward a better way of looking at, and dwelling within, the world. In her determined rage against sentimentality and its terrors, Flannery O'Connor is perhaps the best representative of how the Yes and the No can coincide. As a self-conscious practitioner of apocalyptic, we do well to keep her example in mind as we consider the apocalyptic quality of social satire on *The Simpsons,* as well as the humor and lyrical protest present in the music of Radiohead and Beck. Entertainment and serious cultural commentary, we will find, are not mutually exclusive, and viewing *The Truman Show, The Matrix,* and the films of Joel and Ethan Coen through O'Connor-colored glasses can help us begin to recognize an apocalyptic strain in various superficially unlikely quarters. Without the help of an O'Connor, we're apt to dismiss as unnecessarily oblique the ambivalent tone of some of the best artistic expression around. We might even say that without a certain degree of ambivalence, there is no apocalyptic.

With this standard in mind, we can better appreciate the poetry and prose of Czeslaw Milosz, who can praise America as the home of the brave and an unwavering defender of human dignity in one breath while casually alluding to it as the Beast described in Revelation in the next. In his historical context and ours, the writing of Frederick Douglass certainly strikes us with the force of apocalyptic. He pulls down the assumptions of his day with the tools that, in his time, appeared to have no life outside of his own skull, like Orwell's Winston Smith with a future.

Apocalyptic concerns itself with the stories of the disenfranchised and the embarrassing truths of history. No truck with "Ignorance is bliss," and everything riding on "The truth will out." The apocalyptic power of the truthful word is the driving force of Michael Mann's *The Insider* and Robert Redford's *Quiz Show*. The unveiling of a world going on underground (beyond the eyes of the gatekeepers) is the central preoccupation of Ralph Ellison's *Invisible Man*, while Rudy Wiebe's investigative prose in *The Temptations of Big Bear* appears to write a chapter of Native American history through the lens of "Worthy is the Lamb who was slain."

While disposable pop and it's-so-hard-to-be-me ballads dominate the radio waves, unmasking the old and inaugurating the new appear to be the guiding vision of performers like Fela Kuti, Bob Marley, and Bruce Cockburn. Hip-hop, which often regards women contemptuously, romanticizes violence, and celebrates material wealth as the height of success, has largely renounced its apocalyptic birthright, but Blackalicious, Jurassic Five, Lauryn Hill, and the Beastie Boys are inspiring exceptions. For the moment, the so-called country music industry is a tale too sad to dwell upon, but there's always Johnny Cash, Nick Cave, Bruce Springsteen, Victoria Williams, Tom Waits, and, in his genre-transcending way, possibly the songwriter with the most unmistakably moral discernment on the radar screen, Elvis Costello. Don't get me started on the glories of Bob Dylan.

This is just a thumbnail sketch and in no way comprehensive, but I wouldn't want to leave out the apocalyptic power of performance art, well-pioneered by Charlie Chaplin and exemplified by the likes of Andy Kaufman and Laurie Anderson, whose meditations on the given call us toward a deeper understanding of our words and actions, their consequences, and our transcendent ridiculousness. These epiphanies are constantly on offer in the work of Ira Glass and his cohorts on National Public Radio's "This American Life," whose carefully crafted stories drive us to imagine lives, from telemarketers to kidnappers to evangelists, in a spirit of delayed judgment. I think too of the work of Michael Moore and the ministry of cultural revolution that is *Adbusters* magazine. All of this and more is also evident in just about everything we get from U2 and REM.

In our time, most of what passes for entertainment serves the end that Russian filmmaker Andrey Tarkovsky describes as "the total destruction in people's awareness of all that goes with a conscious sense of the beautiful." As it aspires to no deeper vocation than enthralling the viewer long enough to sell something, the media culture "is crippling people's souls, setting up barriers between man and the crucial questions of his existence, his consciousness of himself as a spiritual being."[6] The experience of a Tarkovsky film is difficult to describe, but, like the work of Wim Wenders and Mike Leigh, it somehow restores the perplexity that arises when we're made to look hard (by looking again) at the world. Apocalyptic specializes in bringing us back around to viewing the world and the people within it as miraculously opaque. When we lose the opacity, we're no longer seeing well. As C. S. Lewis has pointed out, if we were able to see another human being, *any* human being, in their actual transcendent glory and infinite value, we'd tempted to fall to our knees in worship.

When we speak of "God," "truth," "glory," "success," "good," "life," "humanity," "real," "necessity," or "profit" and believe that we know fully or have, in any way, gotten to the bottom of what we're talking about, we've lost it. Perhaps we might say that it's straitjacket time. It, now and forever, is bigger than we think. It is always more than what we have in mind ("Why do you call me good?"). I'm grateful for and in dire need of whatever art can keep me awake and alive to the mystery, whatever keeps me paying attention, whatever reminds me that none of us (and no ideology) are possessors of the final say. Art that doesn't bear witness to the opaque, the mysterious, or even allow any ambiguity is propaganda at best and, at worst, a ministry of death, an exercise in sentimentalizing, self-congratulatory delusion.

While the specifically apocalyptic is always earth-bound, referring to existence *in the world*, it's also appropriate to suggest that the world exists inside apocalyptic. Within the biblical tradition, it is the metanarrative within which all goings-on go on. The Revelation of St. John the Divine (a testament to opacity) specifically presents itself to the beleaguered listeners of the early church as

21

the lens by which their troubled reality is to be read: What's going on, where it's at, and how to get into it. It's the black hole that presents itself as the bigger whole of God's redemptive purposes.

A Word on the Big One

Revelation ("the Apocalypse") is a document that believers throughout history have claimed and tolerated as a part of their tradition (like some deranged relative), but which many would prefer not to think about. Mostly unread, it's as if we assume it to be the obscure clause by which God reserves the right to go crazy on us. Many are divided between the two extremes of either concluding that it has never made any sense to anyone and never will or that someone's finally cracked the code and mapped it all out in Middle Eastern geography and the development of the United Nations. A title like *Revelation Explained* sounds about as convincing (and modest) as *Humility and How I Achieved It*.

Martin Luther once remarked that the Book of Revelation will either find the reader mad or leave him mad. I was intrigued to discover his startling admission on the subject: "My spirit cannot accommodate itself to this book. There is one sufficient reason for the small esteem in which I hold it—that Christ is neither taught in it nor recognized."[7] John Calvin apparently steered clear of it completely, and we might wish that many in our day had followed his example. Eugene Peterson has suggested that it might best be understood by some future generation whose imagination is more fully immersed in visual imagery.

In my efforts to understand it, the most illuminating work I've found is the translation and commentary provided by G. B. Caird. While he mostly leaves it to us to note within our own moment in history the possibilities of applicability, he also illustrates the deeply commonsensical notion that we have to begin with what John was trying to communicate to his sisters and brothers in the early churches. Many were looking at the possibility of martyrdom, perhaps wondering how it is that "Jesus is Lord" when the violence and exploitation that rule the world appear to suggest otherwise. He wouldn't be doing them much good if he just sent them some incoherent missive that would only make sense to audiences hundreds of years in the future. They might be entertained by descriptions of Godzilla-type monsters sauntering out of the sea and cities fifteen-hundred miles high, but it wouldn't give them what they needed most of all: a convincing account of why they shouldn't throw in the towel.

When Caird calls it a prophecy, he's speaking of how John's book tries to reveal to his audience the true nature of their experience while summoning them to a specific lifestyle. All of this not just in the context of what God will do for and through them but also how it will relate to his longsuffering intentions for the created world. In the letters of Jesus ("the living one") to the churches, "they are being prepared by him, not for him."[8] In the paradoxical power of the Lamb who was slain, "omnipotence is not to be understood as the power of unlimited coercion, but as the power of infinite persuasion, the invincible power of self-negating, self-sacrificing love."[9] In following the cosmically effective pattern of Jesus' vocation of suffering servanthood, they're invited to participate in "the approaching world-wide victory of God."[10] The oft-repeated "Come" is not a world-denying programming of destruction, but a declaration that there is no foreclosure, no crack-down, no crucifixion that can't be "woven into the pattern of God's gracious purpose."[11] All dehumanizing practices will be turned against themselves and overthrown.

John's fellow Christians are in dire need of this kind of word. The invigoration he offers insists not only that their suffering is momentary but that it's purposeful: "It is a travesty of Christian belief to suppose that God has no purpose for creation as a whole, and is content to rescue the small company of elect like brands snatched from the everlasting bonfire. John believes that the redemptive work of God, achieved through the death of Christ and the martyrdom of his followers, will bring the created universe to its proper goal."[12]

As the early Christians' category-defying, gathering community challenges and relativizes the ultimacies of Roman power, John's text gives literary testimony to their alternative cultural vision and its destiny as the culture that, through suffering, will ultimately overcome. "The monster that rises from the abyss" is

23

whatever power sets itself up against God's purpose and the believing, enduring minority of John's community, the bearer and instrument of God's good intentions for the world. Evil, after all, doesn't recommend itself to us by growling and beating its chest. It urges itself upon our hearts and minds by masquerading as the only possible way, the best of all worlds, and the greatest good, while fooling itself concerning its own moral defectedness. It was once Babylon, then Rome, but the monster, as a myth, "expresses a perennial hazard in the political life of men."[13] Like every nation-state that sets itself up above all nations through means of mass exploitation and destruction (while calling itself a beacon), its end is forthcoming.

Here we have the clash of civilizations. Not East vs. West, but the "way of the world" vs. "the testimony of Jesus" to which the oppressed believers are told to hold fast. The tension between the two is no less palpable in our day than it was in their day of a so-called *Pax Romana*. The form of things is passing away, the old world is coming undone, and a new one (then and now) is underway. John's declaration that "the sovereignty of the world has passed to our God and to his Christ" is nothing if not political. As we try to get our heads around this reality, we might be helped by William Cavanaugh's observation that "the distinction between politics and religion was not discovered but invented."[14] Such distinctions are generally the constructs of armchair theologians who, unlike the believers of John's time and the two-thirds world of our own, prefer them. Caird describes John's vision as "a future which interpenetrates and informs the present,"[15] a witness, incidentally, that draws deeply from Jewish tradition to affirm its incarnational politics:

> See, the home of God is among mortals.
> God will dwell with them.
> They will be God's peoples.
> And God will be with them (Revelation 21:3).

If we're going to lay hold of John's call to an earth-bound resistance movement of actual relevance, we have to abandon the deeply unbiblical notions of souls being removed from the earth

24

for having believed the right things and "follow the Lamb wherever he goes" as we seek the redemption of our world in the everyday. This will look less like "end-times" mania and more like a celebration of Martin Luther King Day or the Truth and Reconciliation Commissions in South Africa, which put into difficult practice Desmond Tutu's dictum: No future without forgiveness. We are so caught up in a spirit/body dualism that some will still misunderstand Martin Luther King's vision or Tutu's slogan as a mixing up of politics with religion. The opposite is closer to the fact of the matter. Such confidence in a new day coming and the biblical imperative of reconciliation aren't based in some optimistic ideology of liberalism. It's an applied faith rooted in the eschatological hope of the New Testament: Jesus' testimony is true and his way will overcome. "The river of the water of life" flowing out of the New Jerusalem isn't a fiery deluge destroying all things "secular." These are culture-sustaining waters, and the leaves of "the Tree of Life," on either side, are "for the healing of the nations." When much of white America had conveniently reduced the claims of the gospel to a "personal, private faith," King and his public captured the international imagination with a full-bodied witness of a kingdom coming "on earth as it is in heaven."

I noticed a billboard recently which advertised a web site promising "THE TRUTH about the End Times." It occurred to me that the site might have it about right if it featured photographs of people of various races marching together on Martin Luther King Day. We can notice, as well, that hardly anyone complains about the use of religious imagery and hymns in the enactment of this public holiday. In fact, most everyone present joins in the singing of lyrical protest. Perhaps what an unexamined mind would view as antireligious forces are frequently a cry for the real thing: an embodied, real-life faith. For once, the recognizably Christian. Hardly anyone is down on Dorothy Day, for instance, and most African-Americans have long understood that this is the kind of mixing of "religion and politics" that gives Christianity a good name. Christianity as a performative utterance. It announces God's incarnate victory over evil in a live demonstration of everyday apocalyptic.

25

James Joyce viewed the role of the artist as that of a kind of priest who can convert the seemingly mundane daily bread of common experience into the radiant body of everlasting, neverending life. Something of this conversion is present in each of the subjects under examination throughout this book. For the apocalyptically minded, such transformations are perpetually in progress whether we go to the trouble of paying attention or not. The feverish activity of accumulation and mismeasurement by which we order our existence, and which we foolishly call self-interest, is exposed as silly and short-sighted in the light of apocalyptic art that unveils the fact of the matter: The kingdom of the world is becoming the kingdom of God, and it doesn't depend upon our acknowledgement or faithfulness to it within our highly-charged present. It's coming anyway. It is and was and is to come. We have the privilege of watching and praying and noticing in the glorious meantime, especially in what appear to be the unlikeliest of corners. To reimagine now is our work and our pleasure. Look harder. It is at hand.

TWO

You Think You Been Redeemed

Flannery O'Connor's Exploding Junk Pile of Despair

The opposite of love is not hatred; it is indifference. When we have learned indifference, when we are really skilled and determined at the business of ignoring others, of putting our own well-being, our own options, first—of thrusting our own ego into life, as the ideal form of life itself—we may be quite certain that at that point, life has become hell. We need be no more thoroughly damned.

Daniel Berrigan, *Consequences: Truth and . . .*

The only person who can be disenchanted is the one who has not grasped that the world is a dark marvel. Disenchantment is a sign of stupidity.

Hans Urs von Balthasar, *Bernanos: An Ecclesial Existence*

Whenever someone speaks favorably of Flannery O'Connor, I want to hold their face in my hands and look deep into their eyes to see if I can't detect some maniacally enlightened clarity of vision. If you're not against her, you're for her. And if you're really for her, I can't help but think that you've been, to adapt a phrase Faulkner applied to Joyce, electrocuted by divine fire. All of this is to say, if you've read her faithfully, an in-break has occurred. It is, in fact, ongoing. Nothing will be the same. Fair is foul. Foul is fair. Up is down. Black is white.

The faithful reader of Flannery O'Connor will have met the Misfit of "A Good Man Is Hard to Find," a serial killer haunted by the career of the resurrected Jew: "Jesus was the only One that ever raised the dead, and he shouldn't have done it." This isn't a historical issue that one can consider from a cool remove, "He thrown everything off balance. If He did what He said, then it's nothing for you to do but throw away everything and follow him." And if he didn't? "No pleasure but meanness."[1]

The Misfit is not a pleasant person. Such talk of Jesus isn't the kind of disruptive either/or (a "personal, private" matter) one is expected to bring up in polite conversation. But like all of O'Connor's characters, the Misfit gets under the skin, and the offense isn't lessened by the fact that he is probably the most clear-headed individual in her world. While most of her characters pass their time feverishly defending themselves from the unacknowledged conflict in their hearts, the Misfit sees the path before him. Even better (or worse, depending on the fastidiousness of the reader), his most recent murder affords him an epiphany, which is to say that divine grace has just made its way through to him. As is constantly the case in O'Connor's realm, grace rains down on the righteous and the unrighteous alike, and her subject is the grotesque everyone. We're certainly allowed to find this both perfectly ridiculous and horribly "unpleasant," to which O'Connor has one characteristic, all-purpose reply: "One writes what one can."[2]

Though they're all mostly short and entirely unpretentious, O'Connor's stories leave me feeling winded and humbled. Her endings always manage to surprise me even when I've read them numerous times before. As a rule, you can generally read the first paragraph, close your eyes and imagine what the worst possible fate could be for the characters described, and then continue reading to gradually discover that whatever the worst-case scenario you had in mind, it probably wasn't sufficiently horrifying. And yet somehow, with your head pounding, you know that the story was accelerating inevitably to this point from the very first word. This is the way it had to be, and to insist otherwise feels almost immodest. Somehow, you can even sense, beyond whatever it is O'Connor herself had in mind when she started, a voice affirming, amid the mind-bending messiness, "It is good."

This makes reading O'Connor a deeply disconcerting experience, but ever since she came into my life, I've felt certain that we need more of it. She's very popular, and she gets referenced by all sorts of people from Martin Scorcese to P. J. Harvey. But in my view, she can hardly ever be popular enough, because there's something uniquely healing in her powers. She cures the heart of all desensitizing sentimentality. In her company, we will be shocked awake from whatever anaesthetizing spirits have rendered us incapable of thinking clearly about ourselves and the world we inhabit. She delivers us from the deluding evil that is ever apocalyptic's moving target. Listening to her stories changes everything. A new world is busting through the fabric of folly. It isn't polite. It isn't what we're expecting. And it's offering us a choice that we will have to make, even if it kills us.

Among the Damned

Harold Bloom has some helpful advice on how to most rewardingly read O'Connor: "I think that the best way to read her stories is to begin by acknowledging that one is among her damned, and then go on from there to enjoy her grotesque and unforgettable art of storytelling."[3] I agree completely and would only emphasize that O'Connor locates herself among the damned as well, and the trembling confusion to which she subjects her characters is the atmospheric condition within which she, by her own accounts, lived her life: "I seldom know in any given circumstance whether the Lord is giving me a reward or a punishment."[4] She isn't some

29

condescending taskmaster, forcibly pushing her pawns to their assigned fates within her own calculated ideology. They're mysteries to her, and she is, among them, the chiefest of sinners. When she observes that "God rescues ourselves from ourselves if we want Him to,"[5] she isn't professing such principles from the perspective of one who has done an especially good job desiring rescue from this mentality of death. Her orchestrations are not from on high. Jonathan Swift *is* a yahoo. We're all citizens of Springfield. And Flannery O'Connor is one of us.

She invites us toward an amusement that leads to repentance, and among her characters—these closed, idiot hearts who generally seek no revelation—the cartoonishness should not be misunderstood as a detached arrogance on the part of the storyteller. As O'Connor explains, "For the things that I want them to do, my characters apparently will have to seem twice as human as humans."[6] If we understand the people around us to be, by their mystery and utter uncategorizability, beyond our vocabularies or powers of description, then a kind of affectionate exaggeration becomes an appropriate response to one another. Even if a potential maliciousness were to arise in the creative process, it would result in something at odds with what she's trying to do: "It is hard to make your adversaries real people unless you recognize yourself in them—in which case, if you don't watch out, they cease to be adversaries."[7] In this sense, good storytelling becomes an antidote for all sorts of unkind imaginings.

The good story, like anything that fits the apocalyptic label, will jump the barricades of all preconceived and prejudicial dispositions. One of the biggest barriers to proper thinking and moral action, among O'Connor's characters, appears to be what we've come to call sentimentality. It's the sleepwalking tendency that confuses itself for depth of feeling. It's anything that tricks us into thinking we're looking into matters deeply by flattering us into believing our own emotions as the height of sincerity. Whatever drowns out the voice of reality with artificially maintained emotion will receive her keenest cut, jolting us alive like a bucket of cold water. As ever, it's for our own good.

As is the case for her characters, setting oneself apart from the madding crowd, refusing empathy or solidarity in an "I would never . . ." fashion, is an exercise in eternal self-destruction. For the fastidious characters, hell-bent on holding themselves aloof, she will cut no slack because she knows she can't afford to do as much for herself. She pushes them together until they can hardly stand it. When Hazel Motes of *Wise Blood* stares at a stuck-up stranger through narrowed eyes and says, "If you've been redeemed, I wouldn't want to be,"[8] O'Connor certainly sympathizes with such contempt, but she knows that she *and* Hazel will have to abdicate the seat of judgment if they're ever to be saved. For O'Connor, the surest road to hell is occupied by those who believe they're mostly alone on their path to paradise.

Cruel Wisdom

Fulfilling her understanding of what makes for a wholesome fiction ("One that is whole"[9]), the portrayal of Hazel and his world will be both violent and comic. She will put her people through the ringer, because this is the requirement of "redemption-centered" art, but as she wryly notes, "Not too many people are willing to see this."[10] This is the trouble to which Bloom correctly understands we'll have to succumb if we're going to get anywhere. We aren't inclined to want to see ourselves in Hazel Motes (founder and sole member of "The Church Without Christ") or Mrs. Turpin of "Revelation," whose salvation depends upon finally seeing herself as an "old wart hog," and her future in an apocalyptic vision in which even her "virtues" are burned away, or the thirty-five-year-old son in "Comforts of Home" whose disdain for a promiscuous female houseguest sends him hurtling down a raging path culminating in the moment he shoots his own mother dead. In O'Connor's apocalyptic vision, these processes are not far-fetched, nor are they her own deliberate doing. In all this outlandishness, she somehow outnarrates the unbeliever. The grace operative in her stories isn't some added dose of positivity. It's like gravity. It is as evident as dirt, water, and air. Her characters' resistance to grace will fail, and according to her fiction, their denial of its operation is as preposterous as denying the very ground beneath their feet.

31

What will appear to be a trick (though for O'Connor, it isn't) is how you can't dismiss her tales as ridiculous without becoming one of the grace-resisting fools who populate her world. The sheep/goat division becomes one of those who will laugh at and be humorously horrified with themselves and those who refuse. Guess who looks really ridiculous at this point. You're caught in her narrative either way. As Bloom recommends, best to simply give in.

Hazel Motes will try to carve his own path, apart from grace, and it will be murder. Is it such a surprise? What is more, like most of her characters, he won't even be allowed the dignity of his own carefully orchestrated damnation. Even these plans will be converted to serve the purposes of his redemption. This is what we might term O'Connor's cruel wisdom.

The question of its cruelty will obviously depend on our response. In "Enoch and the Gorilla," we might think she cruelly handles the lonesome Enoch Emery, for instance, as he develops a jealous admiration for a man in a gorilla costume whose job is visiting theaters around town and shaking hands with young theatergoers. While he sits in a diner stewing, a strange plan for self-improvement develops in his mind, and he feels himself "surge with kindness and courage and strength." He confides to a waitress, "You may not see me again—the way I am."[11] What on earth might this mean? Is O'Connor pushing Enoch over the edge? If there's nothing true to life in his insane decision, then his next move is without meaning or laugh-value. But there is something familiar and cruelly comic as he stands under the night sky "with the intensest kind of happiness," slowly donning the gorilla costume he's taken after murdering its previous wearer. He's buried his old clothes and now partakes in a "secular" baptism as he becomes an "it," full of newly found strength and confidence and new creation. We might protest that O'Connor takes a little too much pleasure in the sight of Enoch practicing shaking hands with the air and then declaring: "No gorilla anywhere, Africa or California or New York, was happier than he."[12] But there's some sublimity beyond satire at work when, after his first potential fans have run away in terror, he sits in his gorilla suit and stares contemplatively at the skyline of the city.

I read this story out loud to a group of young people in Northern Ireland, and we found that it afforded a lot of metaphorical value on the subject of how we go about trying to please ourselves and impress others, the identities we enter into in the hopes of feeling important. From the apocalyptic perspective, all these self-improving efforts have the comedic value of the gorilla costume. As ever, we're invited to see ourselves in Enoch, but the joke's on us regardless.

Again, the cruel wisdom and the terrible beauty that direct and guide O'Connor's work are not her ideas. She can't explain why her characters end the way they do because, if her correspondence is to be believed, she doesn't understand it herself. She's watching to see what will happen: "I just feel in my bones that that is the way it has to be. If I had the abstraction first I don't suppose I'd write the story."[13] This brings us back to Tolkien's disavowal of "purposed domination" and the painfully bad literature it produces. The story that simply serves to house somebody's abstraction (or "message") probably isn't a story, in the deepest sense, at all. It's certainly a renunciation of divine mystery and the very opposite of apocalyptic. An excellent account of the unself-consciously created story to which O'Connor devoted her life is available in her words of praise for the work of Caroline Gordon:

> You walk through her stories like you are walking through a complete real world. And watch how the meaning comes from the things themselves and not from her imposing anything. Right when you finish reading that story, you don't think you've read anything, but the more you think about it the more it grows.[14]

O'Connor is describing apocalyptic.

The Importance of Understanding That You Don't Understand

For O'Connor, the vocation of the writer will be a testimony to mystery, and this will require a renunciation of "purposed domination" and any desire to make things come out in a particular way to privilege some culture, group, or worldview. The integrity of the story will require contemplation, not necessarily complete comprehension: "The writer doesn't have to understand, only produce. And what makes him produce is not having the experience but contemplating the experience, and contemplating it don't mean understanding it so much as understanding that he doesn't understand it."[15] This is the posture of what John Milbank calls "non-mastery." It's the faith that leads to knowledge. You have to believe that there is more than you can understand before you can begin to understand at all. Believe to see, or as O'Connor renders this Anselmian insight: "To believe nothing is to see nothing."[16]

Take the one called Shiftlet, for instance. In "The Life You Save May Be Your Own," the one-armed Mr. Shiftlet approaches Lucynell Crater and her daughter and holds forth on the human heart and the question of "What is a man?" While "tapping his knuckles on the floor to emphasize the immensity of what he was going to say," he announces that he possesses "moral intelligence!" After this proclamation, "his face pierced out of the darkness into a shaft of doorlight and he stared at her as if he were astonished himself at this impossible truth." The revelatory power of this description isn't possible for someone who believes he or she understands Mr. Shiftlet. He's memorable because he's an enigma, and for Flannery O'Connor, the burden and blessing of seeing all people as living mysteries is the vocation not just of the artist but also of the believing mind. For the apocalyptically informed, it's to do what comes, in the eschatological sense, naturally.

One of her walk-on characters in "The Enduring Chill," Doctor Block, earns the contempt of his patient, the young nihilist Asbury, when he observes, "Most things are beyond me. I ain't found anything yet I thoroughly understood." But Doctor Block is the bearer of news that Asbury, by the terrible grace of God, might come to view as *evangelion*. He'd hoped to die with his existential angst intact, but his prognosis is, as it turns out, a long, bed-ridden life in which he will daily experience the pleasure and pain of the Holy Ghost gradually descending upon him in the form of a cracked, water-stained ceiling as he comes to understand that he, too, is a blessed know-nothing.

The systemic evil of knowing it all, of totalism in all its forms and the sentimentalizing spirits that sustain it, whether in arrogant unbelief or smug, religious hypocrisy, will be brought down by any means necessary. Whatever odd fact of the daily can sideswipe us into a state of dumbfoundedness will do the salvific damage, and the saving pleas of ignorance take many forms. It's as if her stories aspire to nothing so much as drawing the reader out of the idiotic presumption that any aspect of reality can be reduced to the scope of our understanding. The awed silence before a strutting peacock on her Georgian farm is one of O'Connor's most famous descriptions of everyday apocalyptic. She notes that the "galaxy of gazing, haloed suns" will elicit everything from "Amen! Amen!" to "That's the king of the birds," to "Get a load of that bastard!"[17] Whatever its manifestation, viewing any aspect of the world as an epiphany is, in her estimation, a gesture of hope.

Her most poetically rendered vision of a kingdom, a new creation being born all around us, and our tragically habitual disenchantment is found in a section of *Wise Blood:*

> The black sky was underpinned with long silver streaks that looked like scaffolding and depth on depth behind it were thousands of stars that all seemed to be moving very slowly as if they were about some vast construction work that involved the whole order of the universe and would take all time to complete. No one was paying attention to the sky.

"The Weight of Centuries"

In O'Connor's world, the failure to pay attention is epidemic. With this in mind, we shouldn't be surprised to find that the most neglected and the most watchful among her characters are the children. If, as Jean Pierre de Caussade affirms, "God teaches the heart not by ideas, but by pains and contradictions,"[18] O'Connor never hesitates to suffer the children to suffer the teaching of much pain. Her people are dignified with hopes that will always exceed, in every sense, their resources. This is their glory and their rage. I can't think of another writer who attributes as much gravity and moral dignity to children: "The weight of centuries lies on children, I'm sure of it."[19]

"Temple of the Holy Ghost" would appear to be the closest we get to an autobiographical sketch. The child dreams daydreams of martyrdom and distributes maximum sass to friends and family. Her churning imagination is almost like a fever within, but she yields to the scandalous grace and mystery evident in the testimony of a side-show hermaphrodite ("This is the way He wanted me to be and I ain't disputing His way."[20]). She's chastened over her failure to view the people around her as holy, of great value, and as temples of the Holy Ghost. Refined by the fire of mutual freakishness, she will never be the same.

"The River," at points, is almost like a prose poem. It features a profoundly neglected child who is all longing. His babysitter takes him down to "a healing," and it isn't even clear that he's ever seen naturally running water before. A hymn-singing young preacher stands in the river, reprimanding all onlookers who've come looking for a miracle and proclaiming a kingdom that will not be entered into without suffering. The cadences of the preacher's speech and the vision of the child merge together like a dream. The hypnotic language of the sermon commends itself to the child's mind like a song:

> All the rivers come from that one River and go back to it like it was the ocean sea and if you believe, you can lay your pain in that River and get rid of it because that's the River that was made to carry sin. It's a River full of pain itself, pain itself, moving toward the Kingdom of Christ, to be washed away, slow, you people, slow as this here old red water river round my feet.[21]

The child's babysitter asks him if he's ever been baptized, and when he doesn't protest, she hands him out to the preacher who regards him with a seriousness he's never known: "You count now. You didn't even count before."[22] Shocked and confused by his baptism, he returns home to the habitual hostility that feels more cold and vacant than ever before. He has little or no grasp of the significance of the ceremony to which he was subjected, but it is clearly the closest thing to light he's ever known. In an effort to move toward this "Kingdom of Christ," the child retraces his post-baptismal journey and forcibly drowns himself in the river: "All his fury and his fear left him."[23]

Such unpleasant subject matter concerning the strange, violent processes of sin and salvation can tempt us to want to leave the children out of it. But O'Connor takes redemption *and* children too seriously to separate them. She would probably maintain that the desire to create some fictional innocence zone (an offense-free sphere) where neither moth corrupt nor thieves destroy is a deeply unbiblical, even sinful, practice. It's the theoretical tenderness that, mistaking its fastidiousness for righteousness, cuts itself off from anything actually incarnate and can lead inevitably to terror.

In "The Turkey," we have the most convincing portrayal of a child's fury and fear that I know. The boy, Hane, is running himself resentfully ragged in pursuit of a turkey that he deems entirely worthless and contemptible until he can possess it. With deferred hopes, he sits on the ground contemplating his heartsick state and engages in some spoken word experimentation: " 'Oh hell,' he said cautiously." This begins a string of every possible profanity he can muster, culminating in the following:

> "Good Father, good God, sweep the chickens out the yard," he said and began to giggle. His face was very red. He sat up and looked at his white ankles sticking out of his pant legs into his shoes. They looked like they didn't belong to him. He gripped a hand around each ankle and bent his knees up and rested his chin on a knee.[24]

He continues his laughing rant in an effort to, we might say, get hold of himself, but his project in self-possession is a failure. He's left revving his own engine of perceived manhood as the naughty words lose their power and strength the more they're repeated. He is a creature driven and derided by a maddening vanity:

> He said the words over and over to himself and after a while he stopped laughing. He said them again but the laughing had gone out. He said them again but it wouldn't start back up. All that chasing for nothing, he thought again. He might as well go home. What did he want to be sitting around here for? He felt suddenly like he

would if people had been laughing at him. Aw, go to hell, he told them.[25]

This is the serious stuff of a violent comedy and a childhood chronicle of wasted time. The machinery of unreality will not wait on the age of accountability, whatever that is, and O'Connor won't pretend otherwise. She'll do death no such favors.

Getting this business on paper is a religious vocation for O'Connor. We severely misjudge her career if we imagine her moving her characters through one harrowing adversity after another like a bemused spectator. It is an exhausting and demanding task. Given her own struggle with the debilitating disease of lupus, we can know that staying on task was an ongoing struggle, but as we might expect, she also refuses to take her own difficulies too seriously. On the subject of *The Violent Bear It Away*, she observes, "It's a theme that requires prayer and fasting to make it get anywhere. I manage to pray but am a very sloppy faster."[26]

The Violent Bear It Away features the child-prophet, Tarwater, who, like a young Hazel Motes, is on the run from his prophetic calling and dreads "the bleeding stinking mad shadow of Jesus."[27] He'll put on a brave face and fight off the dizziness as he takes a sip of alcohol and declares, through glittering eyes, "It's better than the Bread of Life!"[28] But despite his efforts to starve himself, his black-hole hunger will not be denied and "the terrible speed of mercy" will overtake him: "His hunger was so great that he could have eaten all the loaves and fishes after they were multiplied."[29] When O'Connor names such stubbornness, emptiness, and haunting, we do well to understand that she's plumbing the depths of her own professed deficiencies and fears. She is not a tourist. These metaphysical potboilers (like the work of Shakespeare, Dostoyevsky, or Melville) describe a process she knows to be beyond her powers: a tragicomedy of freedom, necessity, and a terrible grace transcending both.

"With One Eye Squinted"

In our effort to better appreciate contemporary apocalyptic, we can't do a lot better than O'Connor. As a self-conscious practitioner of apocalyptic, her own take on what she's trying to do and whether or not she succeeds reflects a surprising modesty. Looking at her philosophy of life, success, friendship, and overrated emotionalism will present the same challenges as her fiction, and her observations will occasionally lead us into a speculative temptation. We can either connect with her skewed gaze and outrageous confessions or be scandalized by them. Either way, we find ourselves looking an awful lot like her characters.

By her own lights, there is nothing particularly romantic or mystical about her creative process: "I come from a family where the only emotion respectable to show is irritation. In some this tendency produces hives, in others literature, in me both."[30] Her created worlds are her natural response to the life around her. And if the Christ-haunted, charged-with-the-grandeur-of-God twentieth century is her subject, her observations, if they're any good, will assume the form of apocalyptic. This will come through in her account of a troubled redneck who's felt compelled to have the looming face of Jesus tattooed all over his back as well as her testimony concerning the galaxies unfurled in a peacock's feathers. It's what her hand finds to do, and, conveniently, it's one way to make a living. She does not presume to know whether it will be of much consequence, but she does what she can. As for her celebrity, which by its dissembling nature will never connote excellence, she views it as "a comic distinction shared with Roy Rogers's horse and Miss Watermelon of 1955."[31]

She refuses the distinction between art and any other kind of work and accords no peculiar dignity to her writing. Whatever we call "art," and whatever we call "work" will both either put things right or contribute to the proliferation of mediocrity: "I even dislike the concept artist when it sets you above, all it is working in a certain kind of medium to make something right. The material is no more exalted than any other kind of material and the idea of making it right is what should be applied to all making."[32]

An overly self-conscious view of one's work or consideration of pains taken will, in O'Connor's view, only harm the work and drain any energy for the task at hand. In writing, the propaganda that results is bad enough and the kind that believes itself to be on the side of the angels is even worse. She eschews language too obviously "religious," but also notes that the modest language she does bring to bear on the unfathomable will be woefully inadequate: "These are mysteries that I can in no way approach—except with the coin of the realm which has the face worn off it. I doubtless hate pious language worse than you because I believe the realities it hides."[33] Given our deluded wills and willful misconstruals of the life before us, she is distrustful of all feelings but is known to observe that, as feelings go, pain is probably the most reliable one.

This determined demeanor of self-deprecation shouldn't lead us to view her as some holed-up curmudgeon. Her candor is always born out of an intense hospitality and an enjoyment of her interlocutors. Her letters are a moving witness to a life of graciousness. In *The Habit of Being,* we have a passionately transparent testament to the world-expanding powers of friendship in a passage addressed to an individual referred to as "A":

> You always make of me what I would like to be but if I took your notion of me for present reality, I'd be in the devil's hands right now; however, I only take your idea of what I am as an indication of what I should become, and the Lord has never instructed me in such a pleasant way before.[34]

Here we see something of the personality behind the apocalypses and the invigorating encouragement by which she battles her own ever-present doubts—an affectionate expectancy born of hope, most effectively undertaken where two or more are gathered, with a remarkable habit of making all things new.

As she understands it, her vocation is to watch and pray and listen at all times. She often cites Conrad's dictum that declares the writer's obligation to render the highest possible justice to the visible universe. And there is no justice without affection. While such lofty language can create an impression of grandiosity, it's important to note that her powers of expression and observation aren't, in her estimation, exceptional or ever indisputably good:

> I have a disease called lupus and I take a medicine called ACTH and I manage well enough to live with both. Lupus is one of those things in the rheumatic department; it comes and goes, I venture forth.

My father had it some twelve or fifteen years ago but at that time there was nothing for it but the undertaker; now it can be controlled with the ACTH. I have enough energy to write with and as that is all I have any business doing anyhow, I can with one eye squinted take it all as a blessing. What you measure out, you come to observe closer, or so I tell myself.[35]

Her lot is, however, her very own. And while she would doubtless affirm Bernanos's pronouncement that "All is grace," she would also note that recognizing it as such is not, for the most part, easy. It will require the muscular magnanimity of an apocalyptic mind. For many of O'Connor's characters, it can only be achieved over their dead bodies, and she does not exempt herself from the difficulties of recognition. For the apocalyptic imagination, the recognition is a full-time job, a pleasure, and one's only hope.

THREE

Impossible Laughter

An Appreciative Response to The Simpsons

Where there is no exaggeration there is no love, and where there is no love there is no understanding.

Oscar Wilde

There always comes a moment when people give up struggling and tearing each other apart, willing at last to like each other for what they are. It's the kingdom of heaven.

Albert Camus

It is admittedly awkward to champion *The Simpsons* (which might one day prove to be the most successful program on television) as an admirable example of apocalyptic expression. Historians of the not-too-distant future will find it difficult to overestimate the damage done to the moral imagination of Westerners in the throes of television. But at its very best, television can function as a kind of benevolent Trojan Horse that ambushes our minds with the lives of individuals and cultures to whom we might not otherwise be inclined to connect ourselves. As a vehicle of story, it can help create a solidarity with the less familiar by encouraging us to wonder what it would feel like to be someone else in a situation drastically different from our own, thus cultivating the possibility of empathy. Yet as it is, television most often caters to our own worst instincts, driving us to base our identity in what we're able to purchase, hijacking our hopes with the emptiest of slogans and scenarios, and wasting our sympathies on tales that are devastatingly shallow and sentimental. It can even be argued that our relationship with television has crippled our ability to recognize, within ourselves, the need for a better way. We're numbed to our own deterioration. Actor/entertainment personality Ben Stein has prophesied that, by the year 2030, it will all be pornography.

But when viewed generously, surely it isn't too hopeful a proposal to suggest that *The Simpsons* constitutes an exception. It would be too much to suggest that the program urges, at all times, a lifestyle alternative to the reigning delusions of what makes for the good life, but it does recommend a particular kind of seeing; a way of looking at people. These characters (one is tempted to call them creatures) have very little that would immediately command our admiration. Generally speaking, they are remarkably selfish most of the time. They are susceptible to whatever wind of hype or false promise of fulfillment holds their hearts captive in each episode. Their failure to value one another properly makes of their life together one disaster after another. In short, they are just like us, only more so. And yet, something about them commands affection. All are soft and big-eyed and strange. They're completely incapable of hiding their feelings and motivations. Whatever occurs to them comes out of their mouths almost instantly, however damning, irrelevant, or nonsensical it is. But for all their powerlessness, they are all the more precious. Their weakness does not provoke derision. In their loud impotence, bumping through their stories like a bewildered bunch of open wounds, we find them dear.

By facilitating this much-needed way of looking through an amused, affectionate unmasking of ourselves, *The Simpsons* fulfills the purposes of apocalyptic. Perhaps it begins with a humor that isn't contemptuous. Perceiving frailty and inconsistency in one another does not necessitate the withdrawal of honor and respect. In fact, when seemingly endless ineptitude is viewed as our common plight, condescension is hardly an option. As a substitute for death-dealing disdain, we get to feel ridiculous together, refusing the disgust that rises when we see our own brokenness reflected in another and breathing the clean, intoxicating air of a mutual confession of personal screwed-uppedness. To attempt to stand apart from this liberating admission is to indulge in unthinking hypocrisy. It also, incidentally, sets up an insurmountable obstacle to a proper enjoyment of *The Simpsons*. Jean Bethke Elshtain offers a precise diagnosis by observing that "We are not perched on top of the earth as sovereigns; rather, we are invited into companionship with the earth as the torn and paradoxical creatures that we are."[1]

It's a strange invitation, but *The Simpsons* serves as, at the very least, a very healthy reminder of this clumsy companionship. We need reminding. Without it, our lives are confined to a vast solitude in which we fancy ourselves distanced from the deeply flawed masses, perpetually apprehensive that we might somehow get numbered among them. Like all great satire, *The Simpsons* invites us to find ourselves within its pageant. Celebrity guests, called upon to lend their voices to the show *as themselves,* are willingly subjected to lampoon as are we. Prepare to partake in a humiliating joy. No human is exempt.

In an intricate, fast-paced presentation whose complexity often goes underestimated and unnoticed, *The Simpsons* holds up a mirror to the confusion of our age. Its quandaries are ours. Ideally, this culturally crucial reflection brings with it both admonition and amusement, maintaining human dignity while parading human folly. But this process is rendered peculiarly offensive to an audience that has grown unaccustomed to recognizing the contradictions it sustains and within which it lives. Unfortunately, the humility that is marked by a genuine readiness to know and acknowledge our own weaknesses and fears comes no more naturally to us than it does to the characters on *The Simpsons*. Yet without this humility of mind, no story, no art, and no apocalyptic can do its work on us. We walk through life unaffected, unmoved, and forever consigned to an invincible ignorance.

When viewed attentively, comedy like *The Simpsons* can awaken us to our disordered desires and motivations, breaking down our illusions of order, while holding back (temporarily) whatever false gods deceive us into regarding one another unkindly. The categories we use to prop ourselves up and over against our fellows are nullified for one mad moment. We're transported into a carnival realm, an outlandish exaggeration of our own world, not unlike a fairy tale but far too familiar and reminiscent of our everyday life to be dismissed as complete fantasy. Like all good storytelling, it makes more tangible and brings more plainly to our attention that there is, within our existence, an underlying tenderness and value that isn't always so visible in our routines and our efforts to merely get by. This is what stories have always done for us.

Admittedly, it might appear overly generous to credit *The Simpsons* with the power of providing, at its best moments, a laudable attempt at concrete representation of our transcendent substance. It is, let us be frank, a cartoon after all. But if you've read this far, I'm guessing you've glimpsed within the show something of what I'm talking about. And if my overall conviction is correct, this generosity of spirit is one of the practices to which *The Simpsons*, albeit unwittingly, calls us.

The Steeple and the Gargoyle

One image that comes inescapably to mind when thinking through the significance of *The Simpsons* is Malcolm Muggeridge's illustration of the steeple and the gargoyle. It first came to my attention in the context of his strange, utterly undignified conversation with William F. Buckley in what Buckley maintains is his favorite episode of *Firing Line*.

It's not an argument, exactly, and both men seem to be deriving a great amount of pleasure from one another's company, but the stakes strike the viewer as, somehow, alarmingly high as Muggeridge, covering his smile, gazes at Buckley with his Obi Wan Kenobi-eyes and Buckley shoots back furtive glances of disbelief at what's being proposed. Muggeridge is contending that all human achievement, this side of the Second Coming, is laughable, and he does mean all—Chartres Cathedral, the Sistine Chapel, Bach's *B Minor Mass,* the work of Mother Theresa, whatever we can propose for the status of dignified and noble and true. Buckley, as we might guess, is scandalized. How can this be?

Muggeridge: "Let's think of the steeple and the gargoyle. The steeple is this beautiful thing reaching up into the sky admitting, as it were, its own inadequacy—attempting something utterly impossible—to climb up to heaven through a steeple. The gargoyle is this little man grinning and laughing at the absurd behavior of men on earth, and these two things both built into this building to the glory of God."

But what is he laughing at? Evil? Pomposity?

"He's laughing at the inadequacy of man, the pretensions of man, the absolute preposterous gap—disparity—between his aspirations and his performance, which is the eternal comedy of human life. It will be so till the end of time you see."

Till the end of time. This is where Buckley, like a great many of us, can hardly help but hesitate. But the alternative, a worldview that allows for some finalized perfectability of human nature in the here and now (the steeple *without* the gargoyle, Babel, what have you), has proven hopelessly off, even dangerous, and we all know it. What Muggeridge so profoundly understands and what Buckley has such trouble seeing (to the former's respectful amusement) is that the state of affairs we've found ourselves in is really quite liberating. No one, as it turns out, has managed to plateau. No one has successfully dotted every "i" and crossed every "t." And there's a glory in this imperfection. Mother Theresa knows she's simply doing what she can, and this, according to Muggeridge, is precisely what makes her such a beautiful person.

As an intellectual whose sardonic wit marked his career as a talking head for the BBC and a former editor of the satirical journal *Punch,* Muggeridge had spent a lifetime dedicated to truthtelling and uncovering the ludicrous among people and events.

46

The interview takes place near the end of his long life, and his modest demeanor makes it clear that this absurd comedy he describes in broad strokes very much includes a life like his own. The fact that he is no longer with us somehow serves to heighten the comedy as mortality gets a word in at his "expense." He continues: "Mystical ecstasy and laughter are the two great delights of living, and saints and clowns their purveyors, the only two categories of human beings who can be relied on to tell the truth; hence, steeples and gargoyles side by side on the great cathedrals."[2]

Something of this sensibility arises as we view *The Simpsons*. We immediately find ourselves standing before a world of outlandish incongruity and rubbery realism. These wide-eyed, mostly yellow, doughy-looking bearers of the human image are as likely to attack each other as they are to burst forth together in song. They know joy and sorrow. They are seized by both grief and glee. And the further they defy the limits of decorum, the more we feel confronted by an honesty that feels no need to cater to our categories and prejudices. They are perfectly ridiculous, and occasionally, through one child punching another on the arm or Marge gently stroking the back of Homer's hand or kids on the playground exchanging a high-five, we get to hear the strange, delightful sound of this silly-putty flesh-on-flesh.

They can't seem to get away from each other, and though almost every adventure holds the possibility of some sweet escape to a life of wealth within or beyond Springfield, we're never made to believe that any of them would be better off by breaking out. The joy they experience and the pleasure they give us are both dependent upon their connectedness. Through their interaction, we sense something of the salvific value of self-directed humor. Their insane struggles recognize the purgatorial purposes of life's difficulties and the relationships in which we find ourselves. Within the humble context of our common humanity lies our greatest hope.

We're not given unattainable images or idealized role models. Nor are we confronted with animated simpletons whose predicaments are too far-fetched and contrived to ever connect in any meaningful way with our own. We're merely given a sampling of the human plight with all of its frustrations, hopes deferred, and apparent impotence. As much as they might resist it, all of the characters are living mysteries whose efforts to fully express themselves form a kind of gloriously embarrassing failure. They are not capable of adequately estimating their own worth. There is always more to each of them than we, or they themselves, can guess.

The richest and most powerful among them, C. Montgomery Burns, is easily the saddest and least fulfilled. When we're brought to his headquarters at the Springfield Nuclear Power Plant, the accompanying vulture squawk reminds us that his lifelong effort to distance himself from the much-despised rabble, while using them to fund his hysterically extravagant lifestyle, has been entirely successful. To his constant frustration, he is limited by the law in the number of ways he can exploit his minions. He will not be allowed, for instance, to block out the sun so that Springfield will be further dependent upon him for, among other things, the light of day. In spite of his egotism, Burns is occasionally seized by the desire to grace the lower class with his presence and mingle with the commoners. His complete obliviousness to the real life of the town he controls, his failure of memory when it comes to remembering Homer's name, and the fleeting nature of his good intentions make these moments a spectacle of deeply satisfying absurdity.

And yet, the satisfaction we're afforded by the likes of Burns (and really all the characters whose follies are both surprising and steadfast) is far from guaranteed. Viewing *The Simpsons* can be an intensely liberating experience, but it requires a disconcerting task that the viewer might not have the wit to perform. This difficulty is most effectively articulated in one of Jonathan Swift's adages that we do well to keep in front of ourselves at all times: "Satire is a sort of glass, wherein beholders do generally discover everybody's face but their own."[3]

With this principle, we are warned that comedy is, in most circumstances, prevented from achieving its fullest effect. It is our tendency to keep it at arm's length, using it to hold others in contempt while unconsciously exempting ourselves. This is understandable and perfectly natural, but *The Simpsons* invites us to a more excellent way. We're called to recognize and be confronted by our own absurdity. Beneath our delusions of control, self-proclaimed purity of heart, and self-sufficiency are desperate con-

48

fusion, skewed motivations, and general helplessness. Willingly, we're freed from the world of appearances by an apocalyptic universe in which people can only appear as what they are. We complete the purposes of parody by letting it hit home, and I do mean *home*. There is no other way. Be amused, be very amused.

We take in comedy, especially a cartoon, with a false sense of security. If Swift's dictum is correct, it often pulls a number on us that we won't bother to notice. But the way of mirth demands that we look hard and happily for our own reflection. We're delightfully disarmed by the sight, because (for once) we weren't preparing to defend ourselves. In the process, we momentarily occupy a kind of prejudice-free zone where we're not inclined to prejudge anyone. We e*xpect* these characters to have very serious problems like we do. Without them, there would be no context for their triumphs, their tragedies, or their tenderness. We become more humane when we see our less admirable qualities reflected in others and note the mutuality. This law of lightheartedness, when carried into the everyday, has the power to cure (or very likely prevent altogether) many an interpersonal quandary.

The Apocalyptic Role of Carnival

We can note, too, that no group will escape the scrutiny of satire properly practiced. Its spotlight is all-inclusive, and the only entrance fee is some small, personal admission of a folly-ridden existence. As a wielder of just such a spotlight and as a kind of celebration, *The Simpsons* fulfills in part the role that carnival played in medieval culture. Russian literary critic Mikhail Bakhtin gives this description:

> Carnival laughter is the laughter of all the people. . . . It is directed at all and everyone. . . . The entire world is seen in its droll aspect. . . .
> It is gay, triumphant, and at the same time mocking, deriding. It asserts and denies, it buries and revives. Such is the laughter of carnival. . . . It is also directed at those who laugh. The people do not exclude themselves from the wholeness of the world. They, too, are incomplete, they also die and are revived and renewed.[4]

The purpose of carnival is to overcome or provide momentary relief from the seriousness of the status quo, the official, the good as defined from the top down. On *The Simpsons,* all societal personalities are pushed together into a normalizing proximity in which the prerogatives of power and class and celebrity are dropped. Last are first and first are last. George Bush moves into a house across the street, Sting assists in getting Bart out of a well, and Michael Jackson appears as a huge, white mental patient with a shaved head. Everyone comes to know everybody, and any appeal to aloofness or superiority from any quarter is subject to the heaviest lampoon and ridicule. The playing field is leveled, and the forum is open. Our sensibilities are infringed upon by the biblical imperative of an upside-down kingdom. Last are first, first are last. *Everyone gets to talk to everyone. Everyone has to.*

But the carnival moment I'm describing (and which *The Simpsons* so effectively exemplifies) does not require a street demonstration, confetti, or costumes. It demands, instead, a realization we find difficult to sustain. Unlike derision, the laughter inspired by Simpsons-style humor involves, before it can even begin, a personal discovery of oneself as, to some degree, ridiculous.

A moment's reflection should suffice to show that this is a welcome state in which the silliness of self-importance and the burden of constantly justifying ourselves are exposed and thereby lightened. For half an hour, we're let in on a revolution in which the notions that separate people and classify them as higher or lower are given little or no stature. The divisions are shown to be unreal and unsound. Our pretensions are undermined, and we're immersed in a world that delights in depicting the failure of our sayings and ideologies and the mockery they suffer in the throes of real life.

This is the culture-preserving, sanity-saving, carnival spirit to which *The Simpsons* is, by all appearances, hot-wired. As the ever faithful mirror held up to the hope and madness of our day, it shows how our expensive, destructive, and ultimately futile attempts to please ourselves leave us with nothing save the awkward joy of liking each other. We get to try to anyway, whether we're looking at our spouse, our neighbor, or Apu at the Kwik-E-

Mart. At the very least, we get to be amused with one another in a manner that doesn't despise. It's a modest beginning.

In his self-interview, "Questions They Never Asked Me," Walker Percy articulates something of the promise and possibility of the carnival disposition when he's asked (or asks himself) about the issue of race relations in the South. Up to this point his responses have alternated between the hilarious and the cryptic, and his ambivalence eventually yields an anecdote which he offers as a best case scenario:

> All I can say is that it has something to do with Southern good nature, good manners, kidding around, with music, with irony, with being able to be pissed off without killing other people or yourself, maybe with Jewish humor, with passing the time, with small, unpretentious civic-minded meetings. Some whites and blacks are sitting around a table in Louisiana, eating crawfish and drinking beer at a PTA fundraiser. The table is somewhat polarized, whites at one end, blacks at the other, segregated not ill-naturedly but from social unease, like men and women at a party. The talk is somewhat stiff and conversation-making and highfalutin-about reincarnation, in fact. Says a white to a white who has only had a beer or two: "I think I'd rather come back as an English gentleman in the eighteenth century than in this miserable century of war, alienation, and pollution." Says a black to a black who has had quite a few beers: "I'd rather come back as this d—-n crawfish than as a nigger in Louisiana." All four laugh and have another beer. I don't know why I'm telling you this. You wouldn't understand it. You wouldn't understand what is bad about it, what is good about it, what is unusual about it, or what there is about it that might be the hundred-to-one shot that holds the solution.[5]

It might be objected that Percy's story fails to take seriously the evils of racism. But surely there are, in the realm of human relations, spheres in which a perceived (or feigned) seriousness becomes more of an obstacle than a help. Surely seriousness isn't the best we can muster. To return to Muggeridge's analogy of the steeple and the gargoyle, one can seriously admire any number of buildings or monuments or stories of human progress. But to do so in a way that resents any calling attention to the distance

51

between our professed, praise-drenched ideals and our actual performance is to indulge the most pernicious sort of pride.

Enter the necessary, much-needed, life-giving gargoyle. It refuses to take seriously our proudest efforts, the various instances of self-centeredness and idiocy that fall so hopelessly short. That our presumed goodness is so devastatingly shabby is not a cause for outrage, but is, rather, an essential insight of Jewish and Christian apocalyptic. An acknowledgment of the ongoing persistence of our frailties is, after all, the central groundwork for all comedic expression. We need comedy like we need the gargoyle. We need a sense of humor. Without it, we lose the ability to criticize ourselves.

Seriousness, after all, can be an excruciatingly inhumane taskmaster. Its vision is very often too small. It doesn't want to know, for instance, that the person disagreeing with us or whose very existence offends has, as it turns out, a really nice smile. It doesn't want to hear that a Samaritan would do a thing like that. No time for it. We have to keep an eye on seriousness. It can make us treat people very unkindly. As Percy says of sentimentality, it leads to the gas chamber. Seriously.

On *The Simpsons*, everybody's soft and funny-looking. No exceptions. Everybody's invited. Everybody fits because nobody does. They're all weird and getting weirder. Moe, the bartender, is just about consigned to a stereotype when, suddenly, we see him reading stories to children in an orphanage, a weekly activity he goes to great lengths to conceal. The writers of the program are kind enough to violate our prejudices at every available opportunity. The kindness and compassion that works its way between them is always funny but never ridiculed. They're alive like us.

In a flashback recalling the dating ritual of Homer and Marge Simpson, we're treated to a scene in which the two are sitting in a car singing Debbie Boone's "You Light Up My Life" to one another. Homer remarks that the man for whom she wrote the song must be very happy, and Marge observes that she reportedly wrote the song for God. To this piece of information, Homer rolls his eyes and says that God is *always* happy before stopping himself to note that, on the contrary, God is always mad. After dismissing the paradox with a shrug, he changes the subject.

The moment doesn't exactly inspire side-splitting laughter, but it's characteristic of the many probes *The Simpsons* sends our way to point out contradictions and raise questions. Given the mixed press the God of American culture receives (threats, promises, and appeals), we can understand Homer's confusion over such issues as a mirror of our own. In the same episode, the unmarried Marge discovers she's pregnant and upon receiving the news is handed a pamphlet entitled "So You've Ruined Your Life."

The bawdy irreverence with which the citizens of Springfield look upon the world can make of the weighty issues of our day something we can consider and discuss more competently. Curbing excessive seriousness makes us, strangely enough, better capable of seeing ourselves aright. Surely an abandonment of defensiveness and a commitment to forgiveness in the face of the absurd (in ourselves and others) will assist in discerning and practicing that which is most meaningful in our relationships. We have to begin by acknowledging the failure of our categories, a task in which apocalyptic is always ready to assist. Refusing to do so results in much damage. As Vaclav Havel puts it:

> Life is something unfathomable, ever-changing, mysterious, and every attempt to confine it within an artificial, abstract structure inevitably ends up homogenizing, regimenting, standardizing and destroying life, as well as curtailing everything that projects beyond, overflows or falls outside the abstract project. What is a concentration camp, after all, but an attempt by utopians to dispose of those elements which do not fit in.[6]

Is this making sense? It's certainly okay to wince or to be occasionally bothered by the shots *The Simpsons* takes at so many of the things we hold most dear. But we're actually being done a service as we're led down the deeply redemptive path of self-directed humor. We probably ought to be careful about deciding we're feeling offended; it can get old after a while. We become offended in all the ways God isn't. The seat of offendedness (like the seat of judgment) can be a real tricky spot to occupy. Before we know it, it can become a twenty-four-hour-a-day job. It becomes all we're known for, and when we're all caught up in all the things we're against, we forget the beauty of the things we're supposed to be for. We forget what the kingdom of God looks like and all the wonderfully odd characters taking up residence there. We forget to revel in dappled things. We forget we're dappled.

The reigning take on reality is one in which there's only so much joy to go around, in which the individual can only thrive at the expense of another. Life on *The Simpsons* entirely bypasses this presumed law and even mocks it. It never leaves unchecked or unmocked the lies with which we customarily stuff ourselves, but holds in constant contempt the forces that milk our souls dry. While it refuses to affirm the most-frequently-aired delusions of what we're told will make us complete, it does not aggressively dismiss, in a cynical fashion, all that proposes to fulfill. Instead, *The Simpsons* bears witness of a better way of abundance in which no economic class or people group has the monopoly on moral virtue or happiness. An effusive goodness and buoyant beauty turn up in the low places and among the least seemly characters. Self-deception and folly are rampant, but true words are spoken and real joy happens in an utterly undomesticated community where evil never has the last word and love covers a multitude of sins.

If something of the sensibility I'm proffering isn't clear to the reader at this point, I'd like to recommend, before moving on, a glass of wine, a relaxed, unarmed viewing of a single episode of *The Simpsons* followed by a light meal and a time for prayer and meditation with John Coltrane's *A Love Supreme* playing softly in the background. If a text might be of help, I recommend this oddly Simpsonian passage from Shakespeare's *Measure for Measure:*

> . . . but man, proud man,
> Dressed in a little brief authority,
> Most ignorant of what he's most assured—
> His glassy essence-like an angry ape
> Plays such fantastic tricks before heaven
> As makes the angels weep (II.ii.117–123).

The Context of Love Is the World

While much in the way of popular entertainment serves escapist purposes, *The Simpsons,* like all good apocalyptic, confronts us with what C. S. Lewis has termed the tether and the pang of the particular. It does us the favor of bringing our sayings and slogans and self-congratulation back down to the hard earth. By constantly replacing the picture-perfect with the embarrassingly familiar, it reminds me that my ideals and convictions have nowhere to happen but here. My so-called love for humanity, for instance, isn't something I get to carry around in my heart. It has to find application among the weird, desperate people who populate my daily experience. It has to put on flesh. If it doesn't, I might take pleasure in the warm, fuzzy feeling of my personal, private faith, but it wouldn't be appropriate to call it Christianity.

The Simpsons thus functions as a corrective to all unincarnate ideology and whatever brand of moral grandstanding we might indulge in our speech or thought life. It subverts what Dostoyevsky contemptuously refers to as "allishness," the claim of an abstract (and therefore destructive) adoration of all of humankind and all of life in the depths of one's heart. In his novels, Dostoyevsky never tires of showing how the smug intoxication of this divorced-from-actuality disposition leads to hatred for actual people. Our hypothetical heights of affection and goodwill, well-fueled by the forces of sentimentalization, aren't just misguided; they're destructive. The "allishness" blinds us to the effect of our own words and actions.

In an age of allishness and disembodied faith (Gnosticism) advertising itself as Christianity, Wendell Berry's rather commonsensical observation can hit like a kind of revelation: "The context of love is the world."[7] This world is the place where we get to practice our beliefs. And one particular moment on *The Simpsons* strikes me as a clarion call for this insight and also as a kind of metaphor for the ongoing awakening the show, when viewed properly, unfailingly represents. In an effort to enliven their love life, Homer and Marge have taken to attempting intimacy in semicovert situations never far from public view (e.g. the small wooden church of a miniature golf course). In the middle of one such attempt, an earthquake has somehow sent Homer's naked body hurtling through the air and onto the glass roof of a Crystal Cathedral-type structure where the minister has just urged his congregation to gaze up into the skies and imagine the afterlife as a realm magically removed from everything they see and know in this world. At the sight of Homer's flesh, pressed against the glass like silly-putty, the minister hastily changes his tune and urges his parishioners to look down and close their eyes. But it's too late. The offending, liberating, incarnational point has hit home and will continue to urge itself upon them as Homer slides slowly down, invading their ears with a loud, prolonged, deeply human squeak.

As Eugene Peterson has noted in his work on Revelation, *Reversed Thunder,* "All dematerialized spiritualities are vacant lots."[8] The deafening squeak of *The Simpsons* warns us of the emptiness of dematerialized faith and rebukes our attempts to reduce our allegiances to the merely "spiritual." We're left with the glories of the given and the painfully local. The hope of "the next big thing" is repeatedly and mercifully defeated. The characters constantly find their lives by losing them, and the viewer is made to know that they're better for the loss. The dream didn't come true and it wasn't good enough while it did. Joy and freedom (defeated everywhere but here) will only be found in one another, in all things communal, and in the scandal of the particular. No rest elsewhere.

The tether, the pang, and finally a eucharistic acknowledgment of blessing are all evident in the highs and lows of an episode entitled "Bart vs. Thanksgiving." After all hell has broken loose over the Simpson family's Thanksgiving dinner, Homer offers thanks for the food while interjecting, "Lord, are we the most screwed up family in the whole universe or what?" They discover that Bart has run away when he suddenly appears on their television in a special news report from a homeless shelter. Later, when the prodigal Bart has returned and a haphazard order has been restored, they convene again for a late-night meal and Homer ends the show praying, "Thank you, Lord, for another crack at togetherness."

Judged and Pardoned

The Simpsons also has a way of waking me up from the delusion of disassociation. It's not as if we have to strain or stoop to get on the level of the painfully confused lives portrayed on *The Simpsons*. We are they. And our awkward, common worth is to be celebrated. Our woeful moments of self-importance are indeed contemptible, but they are also the stuff of deepest comedy. Learning to laugh at the great distance between our professed priorities and our actual performance is certainly a step towards apocalyptic enlightenment. Wendell Berry observes "that our truest and profoundest religious experience may be the simple, unasking pleasure in the existence of other creatures that *is* possible to humans."[9] The Christian call is not one of distancing, of becoming less human; it is a call to become more human. Perhaps it is now appropriate to speak briefly of Ned Flanders.

A graduate of Oral Roberts University, Ned Flanders fulfills many of the stereotypes of the American church-going suburbanite. He is subjected to just ridicule over his painstaking avoidance of negativity and anything approaching a swear word, and his collection of religious paraphernalia (what has been aptly labeled "Jesus Junk") is on constant display for the careful viewer. The unease with which he regards the world outside of his home and church is wonderfully illustrated when he passes out upon hearing that none of the Simpson children have been baptized. He awakens and, asking why he passed out, immediately falls over again when reminded of this shocking fact. In moments like these, the show takes the superficial, cultural trappings and the "see no evil/hear no evil" absentmindedness of much evangelical Christian subculture and satirizes both.

This is a good and healthy activity. It should be noted that we're never made to feel derision for Flanders and his well-intentioned efforts. In fact, when he carries out the more specifically biblical imperatives like caring for the downtrodden or going to the trouble of being Homer Simpson's friend, his behavior (like little else on the show) is presented as laudable. In an atypical instant of unrestrained admiration for Ned, Homer even goes so far as to declare to the gathered congregation of Springfield Community Church, "If everyone here were like Ned Flanders, there'd be no need for heaven; we'd already be there."

As a kind of religiously preoccupied everyman, Ned is challenged to affirm the holiness of human experience in spite of suffering and sorrow. This struggle approaches a new intensity with the death of his wife, Maude, in an episode called "Alone Again Natura-Diddly." During his grief process, the pendulum swings from a guilty fear to an angry disavowal of God and back again. In the end, his resolve to hold on to faith "come rain or shine" is depicted with a nobility that, until the next episode anyway, overcomes his caricature.

The portrayal of Ned Flanders brings to mind Robert Duvall's role as a deeply flawed, strangely endearing, Southern evangelist in his powerful film, *The Apostle*. I recall a conversation with one viewer who, unable to cope with the paradox of a religious person being portrayed both sympathetically *and* humanly, questioned the film's value with an unfortunate dichotomy: "Bottom line: Does it make Christians look good or bad?" Such standards speak volumes concerning our cultural confusion over the responsibilities and requirements of storytelling. In an interview with Duvall, David Letterman asked, with a puzzled look, whether the lead character of *The Apostle* was a genuine follower of Christ or just a shifty, opportunistic persuader. Asked for his own opinion, Letterman reluctantly guessed the latter. Duvall corrected him: "Both."

Of particular interest to the apocalyptically minded is the manner in which *The Simpsons* presents and sustains an atmosphere in which, to borrow a phrase from Miroslav Volf, "the economy of undeserved grace has primacy over the economy of moral deserts."[10] Amid the humiliating, status-defying, globe-trotting, and even interplanetary scenarios characters like Flanders experience, we're presented with a deeply affectionate view of human beings. As befits a comedy, we're made to forgive these characters for their selfish mistakes even as they're making them. Our perspective is unique as we're urged to judge and pardon them simultaneously. Setting ourselves apart from this tribe of imbeciles undermines the possibility of real affection and genuine hilarity.

To remain aloof is to damn ourselves to a world of abstraction, as if we occupy some ground beyond the offensively human. This disavowal of solidarity can fast become the way of the desperately angry when we identify people by their faults, scrolling up and down in our minds to find out what it was we found offensive about someone. The fault comes before the face, and we refuse to recognize them by anything more than what we find displeasing about them: "Let's see, how did he bother me? What was it he said that made me angry?" Like the seat of offendedness, such judgmentalism is a kind of addiction within our culture, and the television industry (perhaps especially the news media) is rarely reluctant to provide us with high-salaried personalities who will make us feel righteous in our anger. Deciding we're offended by someone is a way of euphemistically declaring them an enemy. It gets to the point that we're incapable of talking to anyone who hasn't learned to pretend they agree with us.

The alternative to being so destructively fault-finding is magnanimity, the generosity of mind that is the most difficult and most needful thing. It's our only shot at real joy. It's the patience that makes it possible to enjoy the company of other people, and it's the only thing that makes any of us at all bearable. In its most specifically apocalyptic moments, *The Simpsons* gives hints of a future in which we might eventually tire of underestimating one another, of despising one another's faces, of being bored with our very lives. What are we until we start to see our own strengths and struggles in the faces of other people? This is the more excellent way of imaginative sympathy, which disabuses us of all pharisaical arrogance. The primary task (the art) of morality is the deep imagining of what it is like to be someone other than ourselves; specifically, the person who inherits (immediately or eventually) the consequences of our words and actions.

A New Way To Be Human

> Well, and the fire of grace be not quite out of thee, now shalt thou be mov'd.
>
> Henry IV II.iv.382–383

It goes without saying that we need more than apocalyptic comedy to order our affections in the direction of *shalom,* but, by its very nature, comedy can ambush us with insights for which we were not prepared while lulling us out of the barrenness of mere

59

pragmatism. It points in the direction of new habits of being by happily toppling the moralizing sentimentality condemned by Dostoyevsky, O'Connor, and Percy. While *The Simpsons* never explicitly recommends a kingdom ethic (Would it retain an ounce of comedic integrity if it did?), the show nevertheless takes up the mantle of cultural criticism these authors represent and frequently bears witness to a profoundly redemptive vision of the human.

In a manner consistent with all great comedy and literature, *The Simpsons* refuses to collapse or reduce the paradoxical state of the human condition. As what might be described as the way of fondness is affirmed repeatedly in the series, we also note that it is the failure of characters to value themselves and one another properly that drives each half-hour plot to some fitful, surreal, and occasionally healing conclusion. *The Simpsons* often ends with a moment of communal amazement in which some or all of the cast are made to understand that the world is not what they assumed or expected it to be. These epiphanies point to a world beyond what has appeared available thus far, calling into question, reenvisioning, or dismantling altogether our perceptions. Among the characters on the show, the most regular recipient of these awakenings is Lisa Simpson.

As a kind of emotional stand-in for the discerning viewer, Lisa is frequently rescued from her own sense of debilitating disenchantment. She doesn't exactly tower above her community. She's certainly prone to find herself in a number of quandaries (although not of the same breed as Bart's), and she appears to feel no shame in her occasional enjoyment of *Itchy & Scratchy*. But more than any other character, she's confronted with the temptation of disassociation and an attitude of condescension toward her surrounding culture ("I'll be in my room if anybody needs me"), yet she will not be allowed to languish in her fastidiousness. In her finest moments, she overcomes by noting the outlandish beauty and infinite worth of her immediate company and succumbing to what Miroslav Volf calls "the will to embrace."

At their mysterious best, these moments of apocalypse (and Lisa's response to them) are deeply invigorating. Perhaps the best one thus far, entitled "Lisa's Substitute," features the voice of Dustin Hoffman as a brilliant, deeply imaginative substitute teacher (Mr. Bergstrom) who, by Lisa's own account, has renewed her conviction that life is worth living. Contrast this with her bumbling buffoon of a father. When Marge insists that Homer inspires her every bit as much as Lisa's been smitten by her teacher, Lisa almost refuses to believe it. And when she's encouraged to share her sadness with her father at the dinner table the day Mr. Bergstrom moves on, Homer will hardly stop shoveling food in his mouth long enough to really listen to her. "I didn't think you'd understand," she observes quietly. To which he bellows, "Just because I don't care doesn't mean I don't understand!"

Lisa contains herself long enough to explain that what she's about to say isn't an emotional outburst, and the careful viewer of the program will have noticed her judgment as an ongoing motif throughout the series: "You, sir, are a baboon." When Homer observes that she must not know what she's saying, she screams at her highest volume, "BABOON!" and runs away weeping. Homer is flabbergasted and protests that the baboon is "the stupidest, ugliest, smelliest ape of them all!" Marge wisely informs him that it's no time for hurt feelings and sends him up to talk to Lisa.

In his efforts to make amends, Homer, in typical fashion, fumbles over his words and accidentally crushes Lisa's dollhouse. When we think of Homer's existence (and the image of his naked form dragging the stonecutter's giant stone with a chain around his neck will do quite nicely), he doesn't actually have much to counter Lisa's assessment. He tries to reaffirm his love for her, but when she still won't look him in the eye, he resorts to making monkey sounds and moving around her room like a hairless ape. The resemblance is revelatory, and she finally yields to laughter before apologizing and embracing her deeply flawed and well-intentioned father.

Perhaps especially in the longsuffering affection of Marge and Lisa, *The Simpsons* bears witness to a reality that transcends the allegiances and demands that make prejudice and cruel self-seeking "necessary," death-dealing disenchantment inevitable, and mirthless judgment a God-given right. On the contrary, it implies another imperative of receptivity and welcome. No opportunity or instance of self-realization that fails to incorporate this embrace of the other is ever allowed any credence or legitimacy. The way of self-centeredness and exclusion is unmasked as a blueprint for destruction, and the characters and the viewers are invited to reorder their lives and make the necessary adjustments to accommodate this incoming reality.

As apocalyptic never tires of reminding us, this is the nature of the kingdom of God. We cannot overestimate its magnitude or its way of defying whatever it is we have in mind when we think of it. Our way is to constantly reduce his way (and being) into images that fit well into our imagination (our way). This is idolatry.

Against this spirit of reductionism, *The Simpsons* contributes to a long-standing operation of cultural truth-telling and mirth-ridden unveiling of folly that serves, to paraphrase Walter Brueggemann's description of the Old Testament, as an enterprise of counterreality supported by, among other things, an artistic, resolute buoyancy. Such enterprises can impact the everyday with pressing questions and invigorating notions, chanting down Babylon in a variety of ways. If grace does have the last word, if all is grace, if it reigns supreme, how shall it impact our regard for one another, our treatment of the enemy, our understanding of what really profits?

While wondering over the legitimacy of this meditation, my most encouraging inspiration from the past has been the work of G. K. Chesterton, who made of redemptive and rambling appreciation a kind of art form. These words of amazement, which try to lay hold of that ineffable spirit within the novels of Charles Dickens, have kept me going in my attempt to praise *The Simpsons* and now point more powerfully in the apocalyptic interpretation I hope to urge than I can:

> Indeed, when it is properly understood, there is something in it that breaks out beyond the limits of mere farce, and becomes a sort of poetry of pantomime; a climax of anticlimax. Dickens is full of wild images that would be nothing if they were not funny. They would be not merely nonsensical but non-existent; if they were not (I say it with some firmness) so d——ned funny. . . . These are things that would simply cease to exist in a really rational universe. They are not symbolic; they are not really satiric. They are upheld by an invisible power and lifted without support upon the wings of laughter; by a power more unanswerable and more irresponsible than pure beauty.[11]

FOUR

Bearing Witness

The Tired Gladness of Radiohead

For quite a while it has been possible for a free and thoughtful person to see that to treat life as mechanical or predictable or understandable is to reduce it. Now, almost suddenly, it is becoming clear that to reduce life to the scope of our understanding (whatever "model" we use) is inevitably to enslave it, make property of it, and put it up for sale. . . . This is to give up on life, to carry it beyond change and redemption, and to increase the proximity of despair.

Wendell Berry
Life Is A Miracle: An Essay Against Modern Superstition

It is increasingly being acknowledged that the simple pragmatic determinism with which so much recent thinking has considered social and political ethics, as nothing but the calculation of how to bring the most effective institutional power to bear toward the attainment of obvious short- and medium-range goals, represents a truncated and hope-less vision of the human condition. The mechanistic vision of the social process which is presupposed in the moral justification of violence in the interest of "justice" is correlated in a deep cultural way with a world view which has written off both divine agency and human freedom. The world view which writes off divine agency and human freedom is the self-evident world view of those who today are in control. Apocalyptic literature is written by and for the others.

John Howard Yoder,
"Twenty Years Later," an epilogue to *The Politics of Jesus*

It isn't easy to exaggerate the proximity of despair when looking down the barrel of Old Mechanical. And for those of us who, for the moment, happen to be sitting on top of the heap in the mechanistic visions that presumably run the world, any effort to empathize with those who aren't in the fabled catbird seat can be downright indulgent, especially when we fail to recognize our own collective finger on the trigger. We're tourists, in a sense, whose consumption will almost inevitably fund and fuel the exploitation of someone somewhere.

But the seemingly "self-evident" and the almost "inevitable" are among the elusive targets of apocalyptic that, as ever, will announce a resounding No to both "The way things are, are the way they have to be" and "The way things went is the only way they could have gone." It confronts the so-called necessities of unfreedom with imaginative truth-telling, unmasking that which charades as normalcy and showing it to be a nightmare. The work of apocalyptic, however, will be peculiarly difficult within cultures, here at the top of the heap, for which unarticulated despair has become a kind of lifestyle. The playing field will appear to be, in Catherine Pickstock's phrase, "a purely commercial reality"[1] founded upon the reduction of nature, creativity, and human life itself to whatever will benefit and perpetuate "market forces," and sustained by producers whose sales depend upon keeping customers immune to any awareness of the things that make for peace and health. Straining for a vision of real beauty and trying to communicate it to minds shaped by slogans and the coercive imagery of advertising can only begin to be a possibility once some crap-free zone is achieved, some space in which a human voice can be heard and understood. As the jurisdiction of Old Mechanical assumes more territory, one could be forgiven for wondering if such communication is even possible.

"Resurrection is verified where rebellion against the demonic thrives."[2] This apocalyptic principle from William Stringfellow expands the sphere of hope and possibility to include any and every outcry against the commodification of human life. Every expression of "this isn't the way it has to be" and every call for resistance, however modest, is a step in the direction of life. Only the clear gaze and the honest word can move us to wonder how one might best remain in light or what little of it can still be discerned in the gathering dark.

Where Do We Go From Here?

Welcome to the wide weird world of Radiohead. Listen closely and you'll sense the cold, sweet depths of a very strange compassion. Their art is life-affirming in such an odd and unexpected way that I'm not sure many of us are accustomed to detecting its glow. But listening with the hope and expectancy that fills the music might occasionally leave you with the same fright and invigoration that can accompany prolonged stargazing. It leaves you questioning the reigning takes on reality. That's a good thing, by the way.

Like all apocalyptic, Radiohead rewards repeated listening and dooms to madness the cursory look. Although I'd heard "Creep" along with everyone else, "Fake Plastic Trees" (from their second album *The Bends*) was the first song to really grab my attention. A blistering ode to the era of mass consumption, we're taken through a hauntingly beautiful awareness of our collective soul expenditure that gradually leads to the metaphor, perhaps the defining characteristic of our culture: "fake plastic love." I really can't think of a song more aptly for and to the times, and as time passes, the song becomes, tragically, more relevant. The whole album, in fact, is like the sound of the human spirit resisting assimilation by the Borg, the Matrix, or the Daleks (pick your sci-fi). Self-assessing images of sinking, all-pervading broken-ness, and daily defeat are all hemmed in by a desire to live and breathe, to make something happen, and to somehow be a part of living, unrobotized community. There's an ongoing attempt to view science and technology redemptively, but the limitations, as attested in the album's closer "Street Spirit," are always present in the inability of technology to effectively communicate the strained, beleaguered lives that mark our unprecedentedly bizarre times.

More than any other song on *The Bends*, "Street Spirit" pulls out the poetic of the everyday and offers a vision of the street that the street hardly understands. With rows of houses inhabited by faces and reaching hands bearing down upon us, we're treated to something of the overpowering dread involved in looking out an airplane window and gazing upon a nameless village or suburb while attempting to empathize with its faceless, hypothetical inhabitants. It brings to mind T. S. Eliot's "Preludes" and his morning meditation on the outside world of numberless hands raising their dingy shades within thousands of carefully furnished rooms. While the thought of so much life and so much quiet desperation eventually brings Eliot toward the notion of an infinitely gentle, longsuffering thing, Radiohead speaks of death's "beady eyes" upon us all and ends the album with the repeated, despair-resisting admonition to immerse our souls in love.

Amid the world-weariness, there's also plenty of what will be properly understood as jokes. The liner-note graffiti makes cryptic reference to "the soft warm radiance of money," and their laments are never without a certain degree of humor. "Nice Dream" anticipates the pretense-laden existence of a Truman Show life with a lullaby deludedness. It allows itself a raucous interruption before resuming its chant of an ignorant, world-denying bliss. Tellingly enough, *The Bends* is dedicated to the late Bill Hicks, an American comedian (most appreciated overseas) whose rants against the false and the fake would climax with such passionate appeals to real love and mercy that the audience was left breathless and uncertain as to what they'd just undergone. This, too, is a very good thing.

Slow Down

When viewing, reading, or listening to apocalyptic expression, it's always useful to keep in mind the difference between pessimism and realism in the service of truthfulness. There is a disillusionment that revels in self-satisfied navel-gazing and the insistence that there is no warmth or comfort to be found, but there's another kind (often mistaken for cynicism) that is merely holding out for the real thing. This "holding out" can become a kind of vocation in itself and will involve the cultivation of an alternative consciousness. John Howard Yoder speaks of how the follower of Jesus is called to "maintain a sense of reality running against the stream of the unquestioningly accepted commonplaces of the age."[3] This is a twenty-four-hour-a-day job. It is also the deeply moral business of art. We do well to view Radiohead's work as an advocate in all efforts at increased understanding, redemptive response, and discerning engagement of this wide-open world. Ladies and gentlemen: *OK Computer.*

We might view the title as the band's way of proclaiming the so-called "digital revolution" merely satisfactory, or a challenge (i.e. "Okay Computer, prepare to meet thy doom") or perhaps even resignation of the "Alright, you win. . . . But I'll be back" sort. Pink Floyd comparisons abound, because hardly anyone knows what exactly to do with music this big and intricate and weird. The album opens with sleigh bells and guitars and drums that pummel the listener in a song called "Airbag." Lead singer Thom Yorke conjectures that if he'd been spared certain death in a fiery car crash through the serendipity of airbag technology, he would surely take the time to run up and down the highway exulting over his good fortune. Bursting into a born-again state via a "jacknifed juggernaut," it's as if the assimilation has occurred, but the individual has emerged, in spite of all the circuits and metallic implants, miraculously alive and aware. Though helplessly wired and constantly under the pseudo-omniscient gaze of a totalitarian consumerism, all is not lost. Perhaps resistance can be carried on behind enemy lines. Call it an infiltration. Amid wars on terrorism, natural disasters, and neon armaggedon, he is "back to save the universe." This is crazy and very familiar. From here on out,

67

the indisputable value of human life will be measured against the humdrum currency of corporate culture, shopping malls, and whatever most predominantly foists itself upon us, from whatever quarter, as the purported "good life."

"Progress" is a very flexible word that, like "realistic," can be put to almost any outrageous use, and Radiohead manages to call into question whatever form it assumes. "Subterranean Homesick Alien" features a winsome UFO enthusiast wanting desperately to be abducted. He imagines aliens observing our lives in a disinterested fashion while making home movies of "weird creatures who lock up their spirits" while drilling holes in themselves and living for and through their secret fantasies. The diatribe of "Paranoid Android" proclaims against the presumed integrity of the upwardly mobile whose ambitions only make life (especially their own) nauseatingly ugly. "Let Down" poetically outlines the generational character description of the hysterical and mostly useless young and restless whose constant movement only delivers maximized emptiness of feeling. But before ending with a single guitar strum that overcomes the melodic and masterfully programmed beep-upon-beep, the song offers the modest comfort that one day, even with the world collapsing, we will know where we are.

The final three tracks of *OK Computer* are a wonder sufficient unto themselves. "No Surprises" sympathizes with all situations seemingly irredeemable in a manner similar to that of REM's "Everybody Hurts" with an added dose of the Velvet Underground's "Sunday Morning." With a heart like a landfill and a job that's indistinguishable from a well-paid, slow motion suicide, the listener is invited to topple the government that no longer speaks for actual people. It's all expressed in a plaintive, disarming sweetness, followed by "Lucky," which looks hard at the prospects of mutually assured destruction with little or no distinction between the personal and the political while pleading for redemption and rescue. And we close with "The Tourist," which begins with the unpleasantness of being the odd man out, the one at whom the dogs are barking, and ends with an affectionate word of admonition to the life described, lamented, and celebrated throughout the album to slow down.

This is staggeringly beautiful music that enriches the understanding. It serves as a soundtrack for the lives of people existing under a mostly unnamed duress in what is currently referred to as the civilized world. Need we add at this point that apocalyptic does the naming?

Before moving on to the glories of *Kid A* and *Amnesiac,* it might be helpful to look at one more song from *OK Computer.* "Climbing Up the Walls" appears on the surface to be the rantings of a stalker or a psycho-killer whose powers of surveillance and domination over the victim have reached an extreme. While claiming to be the very key that will unlock the front door, the speaker also suggests that a closer look, within or without, will only yield his reflection. This adversary's abilities eventually take a turn for the near supernatural as he (or "it") achieves a maddening ubiquity through his skull-occupying, wall-climbing ability. The enemy is here and he is surreal, we might say, and only the apocalyptic language of the New Testament (or perhaps a David Lynch dream vision) can begin to nail him down. To return to Orwell's *1984* metaphor of the boot on the face, this hostile force will assume many manifestations to achieve its ends. In the case of "Climbing Up the Walls," for instance, the narrator might very well be, among other things, the coercive, imagination-occupying presence of television. But lest the "us vs. them" mentality erect a defense against self-criticism, the real terror of the song is the notion that the monster (whatever its form) has its origin and its most constant residence in the recesses of the human heart. This is the terrorist within. While *OK Computer* succeeds in marking out the territory, *Kid A* and *Amnesiac,* recorded simultaneously, feature Radiohead going even further in identifying and waging war upon this elusive yet omnipresent enemy.

"We're powerless because we can't name it."

Kid A is a mood-altering substance. At times, the human is barely discernible over the technological, but when it does break through, it's as if we're being introduced to a new understanding of triumph, a glimpse of a spark. The opening track, "Everything In Its Right Place," is like listening to the world groaning and groping for just such a state. Within the thick, overriding organ sound (which can have you feeling as if your head's encased in styrofoam), we hear

69

the groggy, wrestling realization that we woke up to find ourselves sucking a lemon, suggesting that everything that brought comfort and satisfaction up until this moment is now unveiled as an inimical lie. All the same, this confession is supplanted by the constant, anticipatory declaration of everything slowly making its way into its right place. Toward the end, we can hear Thom Yorke's voice distorted into a kind of machine-gun fire in the background, stopped intermittently by the chik-chik sound of reloading. This is an unexpected method of warfare, to say the least, and without dipping too deeply into that most popular piece of apocalyptic literature, we can observe that St. John's vision of "the Son of Man" includes the disarming image of the "sharp, two-edged sword" coming out of the mouth of "his face," which "was like the sun shining with full force." He also describes the two witnesses whose words are like fire pouring from their mouths, consuming their enemies. Speech is here recognized as the most effective (and ultimately victorious) kind of firepower, and John's immediate audience, the soon-to-be-persecuted churches of Asia, are assured that they will overcome, not through the sword, but by the way of suffering servanthood and "the word of their testimony."

Cultivating a spirit of resistance in a world under siege appears to be at the top of Radiohead's agenda. In an issue of *Mojo*, Thom Yorke speaks deprecatingly of his role in their work while showing little secrecy regarding his motivation: "The lyrics are gibberish but they come out of ideas I've been fighting for ages about how people are basically just pixels on a screen, unknowingly serving this higher power which is manipulative and destructive, but we're powerless because we can't name it."[4]

The power of naming this "higher power" is palpable in *Kid A*'s most aggressive push, "The National Anthem." In the annals of peace-waging rockers, it should be placed alongside U2's "Bullet the Blue Sky" and REM's "Orange Crush." A hard-driving bass and some jazz band accompaniment lend authority to the declaration that all are possessed by "the fear," whose tenacious hold is everywhere. The announcement of the fear's presence eventually becomes a feverish cry repeated over a funked-up jazz cacophony which gradually segues into the soaring strings and magisterial detachment of "How To Disappear Completely."

The haunting sounds, Vangelis-type atmosphere, and sustained Stanley Kubrick vibe of "How To Disappear Completely" have afforded me one of my most beloved instances of serendipitous, creative misinterpretation. Given the usual concerns of their work, all I could imagine with the speaker's insistence that he doesn't exist, that what's before his eyes isn't actually happening, and that he isn't long for this world was the plight of Kosovo's refugees and the prodigious numbers of people, then and now, who are written off as expendable, the "collateral damage" of the two-thirds world as well as the faceless numbers of target markets. This is what Oliver O'Donovan has recognized as a central and unique preoccupation of the Jewish prophet, "the isolated sufferer,"[5] and giving a voice to the voiceless struck me as a vocation Radiohead wouldn't necessarily eschew. Unlike propaganda, apocalyptic happily lends itself to a variety of accidentally helpful readings. To my surprise, I later read that the lyric was borne out of Yorke's attempt to heed the advice of Michael Stipe on how to overcome preperformance jitters just before a show in Dublin. All the same, I imagine Radiohead would be happy enough with my misinterpretation (as a lesson, certainly, in the importance of never letting the artist's commentary get in the way of one's experience of the art), and my own take on the song, which I prefer to maintain, was reasonably inspired by my staring at and thinking about the cover of the album.

Apart from setting the interpretive mind to dreaming, the imagery in the album artwork of *Kid A* gives some indication of "the fear" at work in "National Anthem" and creeping through every song. The painting on the cover is allegedly inspired by reports of fires in the snow-capped mountains of Kosovo. The image gives the impression of having been digitized in such a way that it calls to mind real life being manipulated for the purposes of a computer screen, as if the pain of the real world beyond NATO's jurisdiction, from the perspective of your average Radiohead listener (and the practitioners of virtual war), is about as real and pressing as a video game. The disc, the liner notes, and the website all repeatedly display the unassuming icon of what appears to be a swimming pool full of blood. It is reported that the CIA uses this symbol as shorthand (each pool representing the blood of 50,000 people) for estimating the acceptable number of casualties in particular atroci-

71

ties around the world. With phrases like "the bloody power of kings" and "we're all on the market now" strewn across the CD's leaflet, Radiohead's protest against all forces antihuman becomes one of the clearest motivations behind their work. Ironically enough, they are often dismissed as "too negative."

But this is always the case with apocalyptic expression. It tells us what we're trying with all our might to forget. It shows us the multifaceted ways in which we've become morally bankrupt and emotionally numb. We've fallen a considerable distance when we can only recognize such work as depressing. What could be more depressing than entertainment that serves as a kind of soul anesthetic, broken cisterns that will hold no water, sentimental bubbles that distract us long enough to make us forget whatever it was that had us wondering (for one saving moment) what was wrong.

When we're made to wonder again, we're being rendered a service. Otherwise, we remain asleep to the forces that are milking us dry. To a drumbeat that evokes tribal warfare and an opening croon laden with grief for the living dead, *Kid A* gives us "Optimistic," whose buzzing flies and circling vultures mark off the territory of commodification, where big fish eat little fish and the wealthy demand their escalating share-holdings at any cost. I suspect Radiohead would be among the last to wish upon anyone a culture in which the most visible voice of moral outrage over corporate exploitation of the poor (who make the products) and the weak-minded (who pay the millions of dollars in advertising by buying them) would be a rock and roll band, but here we are. The confused, violently jerked-around marionette the song describes is just as likely a self-description as a comment on postmodern man, because the copyright, manufacturing, and distribution of Radiohead are all under EMI Records Inc. The irony abounds. And the trapdoors are around every corner.

Devil at Work

As their publicity and liner notes make abundantly clear, *Amnesiac* is cut from the same material as *Kid A*. "Packt Like Sardines in a Crushd Tin Box" opens the album with the sound of what could be a white-collar worker attempting a tribal rhythm on the railing of a stairwell in an office building. With an anxious sense of waiting for something to happen (and nothing coming), it features the hopeful declaration that we've sought fulfillment in the wrong place, but it is continuously cut off by the angry chorus that contrasts such open-ended repentance with the call to be "a reasonable man." This is the maddening voice of "the bottom line," which can't afford to doubt itself. Like a kind of sonic exorcism, *Amnesiac* labors to sort the voices out and get each in its right place. This operation is most clearly discerned in "Dollars and Cents," which begins with an unnamed principality calmly urging the listener to be more "constructive" and to "quiet down" while insisting that to really live "in a business world" is probably beyond most. But suddenly it's as if the multiheaded creature has suddenly thrown aside its disguise, unmasked itself, and abandoned all pretense as it chants of "dollars and cents"and "pounds and pence," and proclaims its intention to crack our little souls.

While the world system is portrayed in the most horrific, oppressive terms available to Radiohead, they don't hesitate to identify their own weapons of artistic expression and truth-telling as equally fierce. The language of this unconventional warfare persists in "You and Whose Army?" which consists of what sounds like a black gospel quartet crooning out a bleary taunt through an interstellar transmission against the "Holy Roman Empire." The album artwork features what appear to be weeping minotaurs, constellations, and a possible suggestion of victory one day assured in the cryptic appearance of an Edward Gibbon reference, "The Decline and Fall of the Roman Empire: Volume II." When allusions to being fed to the lions and turning the other cheek begin to appear, one can be forgiven for wondering if they're not locating themselves in history somewhere alongside that Jewish messianic movement that *did* bring down the Roman Empire without lifting a sword. Or in more recent *and* ancient terms, we have the thinly veiled connection to the African-American spiritual "Swing Low, Sweet Chariot" in which a culture enslaved managed to recognize its own hope in the Exodus story (inherited from the professed faith of their captors, oddly enough) of Israel being led out of Egypt: "Looked over Jordan/ What did I see/ Coming for to carry

73

me home/ A band of angels coming after me." The aptly titled "Pyramid Song" reworks these lines into something a little more sci-fi and dreamy involving "black-eyed angels" swimming in the heavens. The recollected vision describes a realm of "nothing to fear and nothing to doubt."

Admittedly, these little affirmations come through in fragments, much like the unanticipated moments of clarity and conviction that come and go amid the confusion of our age. But with Radiohead's usual restraint and subtlety, "I Might Be Wrong" offers a thread of hope that, I believe, epitomizes their measured optimism as well as why they bother with all of this in the first place. Opening up, letting the air in, and starting over are the possible responses to the uncertain glimpse of "a light coming on." While they seem relatively certain that we're in no danger of overestimating the mess we're in, they're also demonstrating, with the expenditure of their own energy, that a new day is foreseeable and indeed on the way.

Radiohead's assessment of various global crises doesn't suggest that solutions are easily formulated or applied, but they are unrelenting in their condemnation of any cynical posture that views complicity as a fact of life, God's will, or "just the way things are." In articulating an alternative space, or what we might call a "counter-reality," they seem to have stumbled upon an apocalyptic vocation. The passion behind the "gibberish" comes through in this excerpt from a Thom Yorke interview in *New Music Express:*

> I read some journalist recently lecturing the anti-globalisation lobby, saying, "This is the way capitalism works, all capitalism is exploitation and to make it try and do something else, it's never gonna happen." And it's like, yeah, but where does that leave us? This is somehow God's will? All this? It's God's will that we sit in traffic? It's God's will that millions of people are gonna die this year because of some outmoded economic policies? No, it's not! It's like some deranged sacrificial altar, the high priests of the global economy holding up these millions of children each year, like (arms aloft) "We wish to please you! Oh gods of free trade!" . . . If there is a Devil at work, then he rests in institutions and not in individuals. Because the beauty of institutions is that any individual can abdi-

cate responsibility. The assumption that we're all utterly powerless, that's the Devil at work.[6]

On the subject of human life laid upon the sacrificial altar, I believe I've found what I thought I'd found in "How To Disappear Completely" in the representation of the isolated sufferer in "Spinning Plates." In a voice that appropriately suffers distortion, we have the speech of the marginalized trying and failing to get through to the power constellations whose interests are elsewhere. The "pretty speeches" of self-congratulating powermongers will mean little to those who are "cut to shreds" in the gears of Old Mechanical. It's the task of apocalyptic to proclaim, by whatever medium is available, who and what are being left behind in the path of "progress" while insisting that it doesn't have to be this way. The song is a forcible reminder of what is *really* happening on behalf of the mostly off-camera discarded who are "floating down the muddy river" while the rest of us are getting and spending and feeling bored in our worlds of mass hypnosis.

Very Resurrection

While I've declined discussion of the videos thus far, I can't resist the mention of a related theme in the Thom Yorke/DJ Shadow collaboration, "Rabbit in Your Headlights," which takes place under the Unkle moniker. Right up there with Homer Simpson dragging his stone of shame, the video features what I take to be an apocalyptic metanarrative for the age in the image of a homeless man, apparently schizophrenic, stumbling down a busy interstate tunnel while being struck and thrown repeatedly by passing automobiles. The pattern of being knocked down and getting up again comprises the majority of the video, and the graphic nature of the pummeling he suffers is exhausting to watch. But the final moment contains an entirely unanticipated gesture. Just as the final automobile is coming in for the kill, a look of clarity and knowingness appears on the homeless man's face. He stands up straight and stretches out his arms in the posture of the crucified. The speeding automobile crashes into his now invincible body, destroying itself on impact. In a gesture of witness-bearing surrender, he is whole and unbreakable.

This image and the moral discernment at work, from lyrics to sounds to graphic designs, are what I take to be the aesthetic might of Radiohead. Apocalyptic tells it like it is. Would we have it any other way? As Albert Camus has pointed out, crushing truths will somehow perish by being acknowledged, and the victory of the truthful word, the story honestly told, and the lies confronted are already present wherever the acknowledgment takes place. This is the way the principalities and powers are engaged. The block-rocking beats of *Kid A*'s "Idioteque" speak back to the media saturation that shamelessly targets the adolescent imagination in a world of "everything all of the time" with no reigning moral standard at all save taking the money and being on your way. Any society whose bottom line is only financial growth will come to view human beings as a commodity whose brain space equals market space. "Morning Bell" observes how a policy of profit over people ("politically" *and* "personally") leads inevitably to the practice of cutting the kids in half. Nearing the end, a tune called "Motion Picture Soundtrack" (complete with harps and accordion) depicts what could be a child of our time, now a world-weary adult, waking up with a hangover and observing dimly that nothing's like the movies and that he was raised on a diet of "little white lies." Though it's spoken within the context of what would appear to be defeat, we get to recognize the dignity of human speech, saying "This is what happened to us," and "This is what was done." Through whatever strange language will get our attention, the job of apocalyptic is to get us thinking hard in the direction of "This is what it means . . ."

Kid A doesn't exactly end with "Motion Picture Soundtrack." Having served as tour guides in a world that will only take notice of that which can be weighed, measured, and calculated (and thereby imagining that these are the only things that exist), we're given a few seconds of transcendence. After witnessing the nightmare, an opening is dared, letting in a certain slant of light that the nightmare, predictably enough, could neither know nor comprehend. The conspiracy of hope is underway, and the fabric of folly is somehow slowly falling apart at the seams. Following a moment of silence, we're given a few seconds of something that always gets me thinking of the end of *2001: A Space Odyssey*. There is what sounds like an orchestra warming up that suddenly gives way to a kind of warbling cosmic sound. Ever discerning, my wife walked by while I was listening to it and remarked, "That's very beautiful. Very resurrection." She was right.

FIVE

Living in Fiction

The Matrix, The Truman Show, and *How to Free Your Mind*

Information theory; it is noise driving out signal. But it is noise posing as signal so you do not even recognize it as noise. The intelligence agencies call it disinformation, something the Soviet bloc relies on heavily. If you can float enough disinformation into circulation you will totally abolish everyone's contact with reality, probably your own included.

Philip K. Dick, *The Transmigration of Timothy Archer*

Propaganda *makes up our mind* for us, but in such a way that it leaves us the sense of pride and satisfaction of men who have made up their own minds. And in the last analysis, propaganda achieves this effect *because we want it to*. This is one of the few real pleasures left to modern man: this illusion that he is thinking for himself when, in fact, someone else is doing his thinking for him.

Thomas Merton

"I don't understand anything, " she said with decision, determined
to preserve her incomprehensibility intact.

Aldous Huxley, *Brave New World*

In one of his typically poignant songs on the subject of television,
"Green Shirt" off of *Armed Forces,* Elvis Costello wonders aloud
concerning what man, mind, or monster is responsible for the fin-
gerprints on his imagination. When and how did our thoughts get
to feeling like they're not entirely our own? When did we agree to
this? Who benefits from our sedation? How hard it is to prefer the
pounding headache of looking hard at the world over the blissful,
happy-ending incomprehensibility of technicolor. If we take Jesus
of Nazareth as our historical model of one who resists the forces
of blinding darkness with every word and action against the air-
conditioned spirituality that loves gloss over substance, we might
be nearing a helpful juxtaposition for discussing the radical alternative of apocalyptic witness in our current socio-political climate.
When thinking through issues of globalization, commercial realities, and the posture of the Western mind in regard to how we
view the world and our role(s) within it, I'll offer, for what it's worth,
a potentially helpful dichotomy: Disney or the Crucified.

Of course I'm referring to more than the Disney corporation
and its ever-expanding operation. To describe a mind-set or a story
or an expression as "too Mickey Mouse" has long been shorthand
for a kind of defensive optimism or nervously defended positivity.
It names a sort of kitsch sensibility that seeks to beautify in a manner that feels a little too forced, that finds little or no value in something like *The Simpsons, Shrek,* or anything that violates its sense
of order. It's the trigger-happy impulse that is quick to judge
images, words, and (here's the horror of it) people as offensive or
unseemly. Think of all the paradoxes Stanley Kubrick captures in
the final scene of *Full Metal Jacket* when his American soldiers
march through a conflagrated Vietnam singing "M-I-C-K-E-Y M-
O-U-S-E."

Juxtaposed with this is the vision of crucifixion that should
never divorce the manner of Jesus' death from the alternative
lifestyle that preceded it. The call to love one's enemy, fellowship

with the outcast, share resources, and refuse godlikeness while embracing suffering servanthood has a way of scandalizing the culture within which the call is made. The incarnational ethics of Jesus embraces everything that the Disney impulse is tempted to paint over. W. H. Auden observes that, unlike the instruction of, say, Confucious or Socrates, something about the new social reality Jesus commands unfailingly elicits (most immediately within Auden's own heart) a response of "Crucify him!" Or as Daniel Berrigan has put it, if you want to follow Jesus, you'd better look good on wood.

I don't want to unnecessarily contrast the Disney tradition with the subversive insights of the Jewish and Christian traditions. It isn't my intention to vilify Walt Disney's vision of an Environmental Prototype Community of Tomorrow or to ignore the extent to which his hopes for international goodwill and order ("a small world after all") are dependent upon the Sermon on the Mount, but there is a real world-denying impulse within what we might call the military-industrial-entertainment complex. This impulse is perhaps no more evident in the world of Disney than it is in the world of McDonalds, "Christian retail," a Gap commercial, or any number of corporations or nation-states that seek to protect what they've come to call their "interests" or their "way of life." It is no slander to observe that the Disney impulse is something distinctly other than the vision of Jesus. In fact, we often appear in need of a reminder that the new world proclaimed by Jesus of Nazareth is radically different from whatever advertisers mean by "fun for the whole family." It wasn't on account of his "positive message," after all, that Jesus was executed by the "moral" majority.

A Spirit of Resistance

As a high school English teacher in America, I have found that the two films affording the most metaphorical value, maximum applicability, and effective citation are *The Truman Show* and *The Matrix*. While very few propositions go uncontested in a good classroom discussion, the intense relevance of these films to the experience of your average American teenager is something of a no-brainer. My students often accuse me of madness, but they find nothing particularly controversial in my observation that these films powerfully name and describe the forms of captivity into which we're born and within which we live and move and, by all appearances, have our being. They know that worlds have been constructed around them, physically and psychologically, as protection against many a perceived threat, and they understand that it is an effort oftentimes well-intentioned and always in progress. They also understand that they are a target market whose buying power sustains the economy, and that enormous amounts of money, mind-power, and resources are expended anticipating and manipulating their desires.

They live with the notion that their speech and their way of looking at the world are often the creation of television and market research. They are painfully familiar with the Trumanesque epiphany in which the words "I love you, man," whether spoken or heard, are part-joke, part-sincere, and part-conspiracy. They know what it means to be unsure as to whether your own laughter is genuine. When Morpheus describes the Matrix as "a neural-interactive simulation," they don't have to stretch their imaginations to know what he's talking about. They know. It's obvious.

Although most of my students don't know what a metanarrative is, they have a pretty good idea after I suggest that *The Matrix* and *The Truman Show* are, for many, the most convincing metanarratives of our culture. They take personally the apocalyptic significance of films whose protagonists discover themselves in carefully scripted, immersive environments that create the illusion of freedom while using inhabitants to fuel their own machinery. They know the joke's on them when a voice says "Because we value you, our viewers/customers/clients. . . ." The bright colors, earnest-sounding voices, and lively music only serve to remind that someone (or something) is trying to create demand and move product. They don't like it particularly, but they don't see much in the way of available alternatives. As the popularity of the films suggests, any articulation of a spirit of resistance will have people lining up. As Dostoyevsky observed, no one wants to want according to a little table, and the sense that they've been playing roles in a vast formula of market research, while occasionally consoling themselves with a packaged rebellion, isn't a realization anyone can sustain for long without becoming depressed. But there is something powerfully invigorating about imagining, especially in the company of young people, what it might mean to take the red pill of reality on a regular basis or to weather the storm to the limits of one's bubble and to break on through to the other side.

Commodifying the Human

For the sensitive viewer willing to make connections (or unable to avoid doing so), watching *The Truman Show* can be a little like watching a horror film. With his beautiful house and his beautiful wife, a well-paying day job, and a learned optimism for which everyone appears to be grateful, Truman Burbank lives inside a giant bubble encompassing the set of a television show (complete with what appears to be an ocean) that he assumes to be the wide-open world. His dearly loved friends, family, and neighbors are all on the producer's payroll. Until Truman, Jim Carrey was normally enlisted for his laugh value, and there's a sense in which any other actor in the role (think John Malkovich or Willem Dafoe) might have kept us unbearably aware of the tragedy of Truman's metaphysical plight. We're understandably amused by Jim Carrey in the role of a man who stares into a mirror talking to himself, unaware that he's the most famous living person, under the surveillance of a world he's never seen. But this opening scene, when viewed within the whole of the film, takes on an Orwellian painfulness as we come to see how everyone who claims to love him holds him in detached contempt and how Christof, the "televisionary" who's choreographed his reality, would rather kill him than allow an escape out from under his gaze. Christof murders to dissect.

As one castmember assures the Truman-viewing public, "Nothing you see on the show is fake. It's merely controlled." Over twenty-nine years, Truman has been trained in the skill of yukking it up for the cameras that inundate his existence without knowing what was happening. The totalitarian product placement and invisibly coercive expectation that he would, at all times, put on a brave face have, thus far, gone largely undiscerned and unchallenged. The emptiness in the practiced, routine gesture feels perfectly natural, and Truman lacks the vocabulary or the vision to call it emptiness. But suddenly, the heavens have opened and mercy has vouchsafed Truman an apocalypse in the form of a light fixture plunging out of the skydome that encircles his world. This is the first of many an atmospheric disturbance, and Truman will eventually show himself to be a faithful and true steward by staging his own. He's paying attention.

The breakthroughs that comprise the film and the comedy of errors through which the cast, crew, and director try and thwart them will have peculiarly powerful meaning for an audience haunted by the nagging suspicion that many tender, heartfelt moments in their own lives have involved a kind of roleplaying, a fear of some brand of falsity lurking behind the so-called sincere. This isn't cynicism, but it's often mischaracterized as such. On the contrary, it can be an enterprise of apocalyptic hope in the face of seemingly insurmountable odds. But a lifestyle of feverishly defended superficiality will not tolerate any deviation from the artificial norm, and as Truman finds out, lethal force will be used to keep him in line. Until then, melodrama is carefully maximized to protect him from anything in the way of self-realization. Everything depends on such heightened security against sanity.

From our privileged perspective, we're able to recognize Truman's neurosis as a sign of life, an indication that he's getting a grip on reality. But when commodification knows no limits and its reign over all of life is a defining characteristic of the culture (as it is in Truman's world and our own), such signs of life are an occupational hazard. Truman was commodified in his mother's womb, and from birth onward, his existence has been carefully scripted against the possibility of epiphany, reflection, or wonder. The survival of the illusion and the success of its economy thrive upon laziness of thought and the deadened imagination. In this sense, apocalyptic is a virus that could infect and destroy the entire system.

"Truman prefers his cell."

Truman's island is called Seahaven, and it's only upon reflection that its name connotes not so much a harbor near the sea as a soul anaesthetic against what lies beyond it. The world of Seahaven fulfills this function not only for Truman himself but also his viewing audience, whose lives consist of little more than watching Truman live his. But the sea nevertheless beckons, and suppressing Truman's curiosity and preventing escape is Christof's full-time job. As he calmly notes in a documentary within the film, "As Truman grew up, we were forced to manufacture ways to keep him on the island."

We know that this is a wholly mercenary endeavor on the part of Christof and his employer, the Omnicam Corporation, but the publicity, in which Christof has at least occasionally made himself a personal believer, insists that they're doing Truman a favor. Anthropological study suggests that we have a way of talking ourselves into the worth and integrity of our work, and Christof claims that his sole motivation is to give Truman a "normal life," that Seahaven is "the way the world should be," and that the real world, as any rational person can see, is "the sick place."

The same machinery of self-justification is at work within Seahaven, and the manufactured fears that keep Truman confined are reinforced by the ongoing theme in the mouths of his family and friends that Seahaven is the best of all possible worlds. The safety and comforts of home and the high quality of the life they live are their constant preoccupation. This is the obligatory self-affirmation of any corporation, community, or culture, and straying from it, in whatever environment, is an atmospheric disturbance (a "thought-crime" in Orwell's jargon). But again, breaking out of this force of habit is what makes Truman a kind of hero and his final decision an exercise in apocalyptic.

To his detractors, Christof defensively insists that "Truman prefers his cell." According to the Truman Liberation Front (TLF), this is the misguided taunt of a mad dictator. They watch Truman as avidly as anyone, but whereas the average viewer envies his picture-perfect paradise, they view him as a political prisoner who knows he was made for something more. To assume that he's truly content with his status and aspires toward nothing beyond

84

it is a smear upon human dignity, and the fact of his longing to set sail is an article of faith. For the TLF, the atmospheric disturbance is a moral imperative.

The Last Temptation of Truman

In response to the question of why it's taken Truman twenty-nine years to really begin to question and thereby discover the true nature of his world, Christof articulates the quiet desperation within which, according to the film, the mass of humanity may forever remain: "We accept the reality of the world with which we're presented." Like Ivan Karamazov's Grand Inquisitor in Dostoyevsky's *Brothers Karamazov*, Christof notes that, without exception, we prefer the counterfeit, the comfortable, and whichever reality least violates our prejudices and pleasures. As long as our basic biological needs are met and we're told what to dream, we tend to expect (and to actually prefer) the expected. Christof holds to this principle as to the precision and inevitability of a mathematical formula.

With this gauntlet thrown down, we come to understand something of the apocalyptic aspirations of the Truman Liberation Front. Ideologically speaking, more is at stake than the personal freedom of one man. If Truman successfully breaks out of the machine, or if he ever even attempts to do so, Christof's nightmare pronouncement that humans prefer a well-cushioned captivity over the God-given world is wrong. By this point, we're already cheering for the TLF. We've already watched Truman's awkward efforts to defy the routine and attempt the unexpected, and we've noted that the characters around him are desperately ill-equipped to respond to or deal with any deviations from the norm. And if we've been completely honest with ourselves, we've acknowledged that we're all a lot like Truman *and* his so-called community. We cringe on behalf of both parties, because their confusion is ours. We're both rebels *and* conspirators.

By the time Truman overcomes his lifelong fear of water to board a sailboat and single-handedly heads for the as-yet-unimagined border, it's clear that he has chosen the most needful, painful, and costly thing. It's all "on the air," as it were, and

Christof rages at his insolence as one TLF member offers up a prayer on Truman's behalf. A thunderstorm is executed to prevent his progress, and Christof ignores the complaints of his sponsors that he's about to direct a televised homicide.

It is, of course, possible that the careful film viewer, always watchful for the director's more subtle choices, is wrong to view the number "139" on the sail of Truman's vessel as an allusion to Psalm 139, but I doubt it. As a poem of acknowledgment concerning the affectionate familiarity, intimacy, and all-knowing goodwill the psalmist attributes to his creator, it serves as a stark contrast to the malicious manipulations of Christof in his relationship with Truman. And one passage in particular has immediate application concerning his journey:

> If I take the wings of the morning
> and settle at the farthest limits of the sea,
> Even there your hand shall lead me
> and your right hand shall hold me fast.

In spite of Christof's murderous efforts, Truman makes it to the edge of his world and walks up the sky-blue steps toward a door. As he's about to step through, Christof speaks his first words to Truman. He promises a life of pain and disappointment outside of his world, and in a kind of inversion of the imagery of the psalm, he explains that he knows him better than Truman knows himself and that he's personally orchestrated every moment of his life. Most of all, he assures him, "In my world you have nothing to fear."

After a moment's hesitation, Truman seizes on his well-practiced wave and tag-line ("Good afternoon, good evening, and good night") and walks out the door. The audience is scandalized and/or set free. Christof and his works are renounced. Truman exits Egypt/Ur and sets his face for a brave new world.

"The Matrix has you."

What language shall we borrow to describe the length and breadth of our captivity? We can speak of the hegemony of multinational corporations over the human heart and mind, the preponderance of the Borg, or any of the many worlds of Philip K. Dick. More than almost any literary figure we can name, Dick never tired of employing fresh, outlandish articulations of how we go about lying to ourselves. But for sheer vastness and a monstrously effective borrowing from any number of available sources, little compares to *The Matrix*.

Keanu Reeves's Neo is the daysleeper protagonist who, like many young (and increasingly not-so-young) people of the Western world, has been raised on digital technology. By day, he sits in front of a computer screen in an office cubicle. By night, he's his own man, hacking into the early morning hours until he collapses at the computer beside his bed. The search is on, and it knows no satisfaction. It is unceasing. And while Neo wouldn't be able to tell you exactly what he's searching for, he has recently nailed it down to a specific, haunting question: "What is the Matrix?"

Something's happening, and Neo possesses at least the beginnings of wisdom insofar as he knows that he doesn't know what the something is. Everybody's looking for answers, we might say, but in Neo's world, it's perhaps better to admit that we don't even know the proper questions. Most of us are too busy grabbing and accumulating to even pause long enough to wonder or dream harder. We need a wake-up call, probably on a daily basis. For a considerable number of students, friends, and colleagues, *The Matrix* has been quite the revelation. Like Truman, we're treated to the epiphany, now and again, that what we've embraced as whole and healthy was a devastatingly hollow dream. But how can one outdo the fetus pod of *The Matrix?* Plato's allegory of the cave, for instance, certainly conveys the notion that we often warm ourselves by the fire of a cold delusion. But in *The Matrix*, we're conceived for the purpose of being plugged in. We're fuel for the prodigious machinery. The commodification knows no end. But I'm getting ahead of myself.

"The Matrix has you." This message makes it through to our protagonist, Neo, by way of his computer. Its meaning will occupy the rest of the film alongside the apocalyptic discovery of what it can and must mean to wake up. When I first saw the film (on an Easter Sunday, appropriately enough), I couldn't help but think that our current discombobulated generation of Western culture was being given a sampling of language adequate to both its despair and its hope. When Neo is first introduced to Trinity, her words are tailor-made for the lone sojourner who is constantly looking for answers (or less-than-edifying images) by way of the computer keyboard:

> Please. Just listen. I know why you're here, Neo. I know what you've been doing. I know why you hardly sleep, why you live alone and why, night after night, you sit at the computer; you're looking for him. . . . The answer is out there, Neo. It's looking for you and it will find you, if you want it to.

From here, it's back to the white-collar routine, where he'll wait for something, anything, to happen. The Matrix *does* have him for the time being, but he's about to be shaken by what is doubtless the fantastic daydream of many an employee in the workaday world of data entry. As he sits in his cubicle, he receives a call from a legendary hacker, Morpheus, who alerts him to the presence of "agents" who've come to take him away. For one glorious moment, Neo's office space is transformed into a playing field of real danger and cosmic significance. The interrogation that follows his capture is too fantastic, in Neo's view, to be accorded the name of reality. But as he will discover, his understanding of reality has been, to say the least, adulterated.

"You're a slave, Neo."

As an enigmatic sage with impeccable fashion sense, Morpheus sits before Neo with the bemused confidence of one who knows more than he can communicate. He can only bear witness, a task peculiar to the apocalyptic, and when Neo is brought to him, he can only pull out the poetry and all available imagery to describe to Neo the nature of the real. It has to be believed to be seen. Believing a revelation cannot be done on behalf of someone else. He has to inspire faith, but time is short. In Morpheus's view, Neo isn't far from understanding the facts beyond what appears to be matter:

"I can see it in your eyes. You have the look of a man who accepts what he sees because he is expecting to wake up."

What is the Matrix? "The Matrix is everywhere. . . . It is the world that has been pulled over your eyes to blind you from the truth." What truth? "That you're a slave, Neo. Like everyone else, you were born into bondage, kept inside a prison that you cannot smell, taste, or touch. A prison for your mind."

While Morpheus's witness is scandalous, he also regards Neo with a gravity that, unless Morpheus is mad, is the most liberating and invigorating gaze he's ever experienced. He looks upon him as a being of infinite worth whose every self-estimation is a hopeless underestimation. This is the apocalyptic Yes. But it is also a No. The one depends upon the other. Neo's freedom depends upon an ongoing recognition (a vision, in fact) of his slavery.

The best articulation of the No I've come across (by way of Thomas Merton) is a passage from Claude Tresmontant's *Christian Metaphysics*. He uses the old word, "Sin," which *The Matrix* wisely refrains from utilizing, but it brings to mind what Neo will be shown in the image of the fetus pod, and it's about the most Matrix-like (and slightly Trumanesque) definition of being "born into bondage" that I know. Morpheus will demonstrate how the arrogance of their human ancestors has assured them their nightmare inheritance, how one goes about entering and, eventually, resisting on behalf of the real world, and what it will mean to be born again. Tresmontant describes the terrain well, and the passage is worth quoting in full:

> The child is born in fact, into a world of sin, into a criminal world. It inherits biological determinisms, taints, on the physiological and psychological plane. These taints can themselves be the consequence of positive faults committed by ancestors. But the child is going to inherit also, and especially by the education which he is going to receive from his environment, a set of ready-made ideas, a system of judgments, a scale of values which, as often as not, he will not be able to question or criticize. This system of values, in the aggregate of nations, in large part is criminal. It is the reflection of a criminal world in which man oppresses, massacres, tortures, humiliates, and exploits his brother. The child enters into an

89

organized world, on the political, economic, mental, mythological, psychological, and other planes. And the structure of this world is penetrated and informed by sin. The child is not born in Paradise. It is born in a criminal humanity. In order to have access to justice, to sanctity, the child, as it grows up, will have to make a personal act of judgment, of refusal, of choice. It will have to make a personal act of opposition to the values of its tribe, of its caste, of its nation or of its race, and of its social class, in order to attain justice. To a certain extent it will have to leave its tribe, its nation, its caste, its class, its race, as Abraham the father of the faithful did, he who left Ur of the Chaldees to go into a country that he did not know. Holiness begins with a breach. Nothing can dispense the child from this personal act of breaking with "the world." In order to enter into Christianity, the child will have to choose between the values of the world, the values of its tribe, its nation or its social class, and the values of the Gospel. It must renew its scale of values. It must, as it were, be born anew, from the spiritual point of view; it must become a new creature. Tertullian said one is not born a Christian. One becomes a Christian. The access to Christianity represents a new birth. One can then legitimately distinguish between the state which precedes this new birth and the state which follows it. The state which precedes this new birth is the state which the Church calls "original sin."[1]

In my copy of *Christian Metaphysics,* I've written the word "MATRIX" over this passage. It's the absence of such carefully wrought, imaginative explanations in the popular and most-widely aired conceptions of Christianity (the "broadcast" versions) that makes *The Matrix* such a revolutionary film. It gives us a sense of sin and salvation which might actually have some bearing on the way we think about and live within the world. As you might have guessed, this chapter is largely an attempt at elaboration upon Tresmontant's insights by way of *The Matrix* and *The Truman Show.* When the self-proclaimed representatives of "the gospel" have reduced the good news to "how to get to heaven when you die," it's profoundly ironic that a science fiction action film would serve to bring the reality-altering significance of the Jewish and Christian revelations up on the cultural radar. All too often, such reductions make of religious faith the tacit (and sometimes not so tacit) sponsor of the powers that be, *not* the resistance force that might overcome them through radical, alternative, apocalyptic living. *The Matrix* reminds us of the stakes and the costliness of such living. Embodied belief. Were we expecting something else? This is the kind of thing people, students especially, want to talk about.

"Holiness begins with a breach."

Having offered his testimony, Morpheus wastes no time in presenting Neo with the opportunity to begin initiatory rites. Though they have, in a sense, already begun, Neo has to decide before he enters the point of no return. As Tresmontant explains, the "personal act of judgment, of refusal, of choice" cannot be avoided; the No to the old world and the Yes to the new. This is only the beginning, but it isn't too late to turn back. The red pill or the blue pill: "You take the blue pill and the story ends. You wake in your bed and you believe whatever you want to believe." In spite of Morpheus's charisma, the viewer knows that the blue pill is a genuine temptation of comfortable numbness and ease. The red pill is the avenue to truth, the unmasking of fictions, and as-yet-unimagined strife: "Remember, all I'm offering is the truth. Nothing more." Neo takes the red pill.

In a matter of seconds, Neo's perceived reality begins to liquefy around him, and as he touches a nearby mirror, he begins to be enveloped by all nearby matter as if he's being expelled from within like an air bubble. In one of the most horrific and effectively rendered moments in science fiction film, he then awakens in a completely wired state and enclosed within a gelatinous membrane that he will have to push through in order to breathe. After breaking through, he discovers that he is in one of a seemingly infinite number of pods, where the rest of humanity lie dormant, as far as the eye can see. He is, in a sense, graphically born again, but he's about to be discarded and flushed down the chute.

Once the Matrix has discovered his awakened state, a machine appears for the purpose of removing him from the system. In one peculiarly chilling moment, Neo see himself in the gaze of the machine and knows that he is exactly nothing, a defect whose awareness has made him useless, dead to the world of the Matrix *because* he's now alive to a new one. He's dropped into the sewage only to be salvaged by Morpheus's ship, the Nebuchadnezzar. "Welcome to the real world, Neo."

"Am I dead?" he asks.

"Far from it."

"He's beginning to believe."

Allegorically speaking, if the central question of humanity's destiny was merely the importance of being raptured out of the big, bad world, I suppose this would be the end of the film. Morpheus and his crew, including the newly saved Neo, would fly away to some distant, planetary shore, possibly shed their bodies, and know all the while that the world they'd left behind awaits its assured destruction in a big fiery ball.

I'm grateful to note, however, that *The Matrix* is more dependent upon and faithful to a specifically incarnational understanding of these matters. From the very first moment of his removal, Neo is being prepared for reentry. The world has been subjected to futility. It is under siege, which is to say that the Matrix has it under a totalitarian control. But there is a resistance movement, a civilization in fact, that exists outside of the control and total observation of the Matrix. This mobile, beleaguered city functions *in the world*, seeking to free creation from its momentary bondage to decay. By now, it should come as no surprise to discover that this community calls itself Zion.

Neo never lays eyes on the actual city itself, but he does come to know what it will mean to live a life of representation on behalf of its ways. In fact, the red pill was his inauguration and baptism into this new and devastatingly costly but nevertheless living way. In stark contrast to their visually stunning, brightly colored manifestations within the Matrix, the crew of the Nebuchadnezzar are clothed in drab, monastic-style fabrics and forced out of necessity to subsist on gruel. The authenticity of Zion-style living and its quality of being, at the very least, unplugged are all that it has to commend itself over the sensory feast of the Matrix. Zion is, at best, the first fruits or the testimonial deposit that exists solely to embody the new day of authenticity that will overcome the present darkness of the Matrix.

Redemption requires reentry. It will not do, for instance, to simply destroy the Matrix in one shot, because even if this were possible, the mass of humanity remains unconverted and would very likely die with it. As Morpheus explains, "You have to understand that most of these people are not ready to be unplugged and many of them are so inured, so hopelessly dependent on the system that they will fight to protect it."

The paralyzed comprehensibilities of their captive minds require a more subversively wrought conversion (as we've seen in the case of Neo), and even afterwards, the blue pill of escape and blissful delusion remains an ongoing temptation. Aboard the Nebuchadnezzar, we have one crewmember, Cypher (whom the agents of the Matrix call "Mr. Reagan"), who wants to be plugged in again. In exchange for handing over Morpheus, he insists that his memory of life outside the Matrix be erased and his mind be immediately reincorporated into the life of a celebrity actor. The process of dissimulation (against that of redemption) is something we will happily have done to ourselves. We will, as it turns out, pay for the privilege. Cypher understands that regaining the world of illusory sensations will require the forfeiture of his soul. He knows that such a final reentry will mean surrendering his mind to the system. The redemptive reentry of Neo, as with any other Zion citizen, will require a different mental exercise. The action of bearing witness *against* the mind-altering powers of the Matrix and *for* the not-yet-awakened living will be a practice of belief, a mindfulness that asserts what it knows against the all-pervasive force of appearances. Holding on to reality, bringing it in, will be an all-consuming occupation.

"There is no spoon."

Neo's vocation is one of mind over that which foists itself upon the mind as matter. As we're graphically reminded throughout the film, this matter is lethally powerful in spite of its illusory nature.

93

He has to assert the true and the real against the false and the fake in a realm where fake, for the moment, reigns supreme, and where the fake, moving in for the kill, crowns itself with such descriptions as "the sound of inevitability." This is dictionary-definition apocalyptic. Our world is not unfamiliar with the processes that would reduce all human life to the status of the coppertop battery, fueling the machinery of stone-cold profit by utilizing humanity's preference for the Disneyified over the incarnationally redeemed. To the man with a hammer, as the saying goes, everything's a nail. To Christof, an unborn child is a ratings phenomenon. To a corporation, a human is a target market. Apocalyptic unveils another way of doing things. Apocalyptic awakens.

As *The Matrix* ends, Neo directly addresses the Matrix and explains that he's about to do some awakening. In contrast to the limits the Matrix has imposed, arrogantly asserting the meaning of "realistic" and "the inevitable," Neo will unveil "a world where anything is possible." He will make a spectacle of the principalities and powers, parading the commodifying folly of the Matrix before the watching world. He is in this world but not of it. He's about to start us imagining what it might mean to rage against the dying of the light and the pretentious busyness of the machine.

Taped on the wall above the doorway exiting my classroom, I have two drawings, each of a pill, one red and one blue. Much of what I profess to students at fifty-minute intervals is dismissed as complete lunacy, much is forcibly ignored, and plenty fails to overcome the myriad images and sounds that occupy their minds even when I'm the only one talking. They've been bombarded by a multifaceted media presentation before they entered my room, and the bombardment will continue once they're out. The Matrix has them.

But from *Beowulf* to Philip Larkin, we talk about choices, the grids that define them for us, and what it might mean to represent new life in the mass hypnosis of the present. We start small with such seeming trivia as not breaking in front of other students in the lunch line just because you can, and somehow expanding your sphere of respect by kindly regarding the people you're not inclined to notice. These are red-pill decisions, representing a lifestyle the darkness does not know or comprehend. The blue-pill

94

option, on the other hand, will involve submission to hostile forces that constantly generate more illusions.

The two drawings are but one more invitation for my students to a more determined clarity of thought and action. They know that it's a funny idea, but many also acknowledge that it can be a help. They also know that while I want my curriculum and classroom atmosphere to be the very opposite of *The Truman Show*, I'm happy for their exit into the hallway to be viewed as an entrance into the real world. There they can either willfully misconstrue what transpires around them to fit their mind-set *or* receive the faces and situations that confront them in all their uncommercial beauty. The broad path of the former has many takers, and they've long known that the wide-awake latter is narrow and fraught with danger. They'll note, too, that red-pill living is best undertaken in groups and that, on his best days, their teacher is attempting to join them.

SIX

Boogie Nights of the Living Dead

The Moral Vision of Beck

He told her about the alligators; Angel, who had a fertile imagination too, added detail, color. Together on the stoop they hammered together a myth. Because it wasn't born from fear of thunder, dreams, astonishment at how the crops kept dying after harvest and coming up again every spring, or anything else very permanent, only a temporary interest, a spur-of-the-moment tumescence, it was a myth rickety and transient as the bandstands and the sausage-pepper of Mulberry Street.

Thomas Pynchon, V.

The past is never dead. It's not even past.

Gavin Stevens in William Faulkner's Requiem for a Nun

A drifter came by offering to rake up the leaves in our yard for money. We agreed to it and were too busy to notice when, after making a pile or two, he left, money in hand, and never came around again. But our neighbor, ever vigilant, took in the whole thing. He's an eighty-five-year-old African-American named Matthew Sherrill, and before we knew what had happened, he'd arranged for one of the men in his landscaping business to finish the job. Any attempt to repay Matthew for kindnesses unsought is always met with a lifted hand and the refrain: "We're neighbors." He provided the following assessment of our exchange with the runaway raker of leaves: "The world is filled with cruel-hearted people who'll take your kindness for weakness."

Language like this makes me feel like Matthew is a storehouse of ancient wisdom. I thanked him for putting it so well and he thanked me for thanking him. He'll often pepper his conversation with phrases from the King James Bible in the most unself-conscious way imaginable, and it gets me thinking about oral tradition, wisdom as opposed to information, and why it is that speaking so poetically comes so unnaturally to the likes of me, a thirty-two-year-old white schoolteacher. After he left our front porch, I went over to our CD collection to see if I couldn't find something to keep my head and heart submerged in rusty old truths.

As much as I hate to admit it, I haven't yet attained the level of spiritual development necessary to be the kind of person who listens to Harry Smith's *Anthology of American Folk Music* exclusively for pleasure, though my faith does have me confident that I'll get their eventually. Tom Waits had already filled the house in recent days, and neither Dylan nor Cash would do it this time, because, to tell the truth, I needed a peer, someone who knows that the only thing to do with a wise neighbor is to listen and take notes and ask for orders. I also wanted someone whose cultural inheritance includes, for better or worse, images from Hanna Barbera cartoons and the blessed sounds of an Atari 2600; someone, too, who might find themselves moved and inspired by the sound of my neighbor's voice while wary of the murdering sentimentality that's never known quite how to talk about these things. We can look for the accidents, the thrift stores, the unDisneyified corners, but we also have a kind of deranged Midas touch in our minds that will commodify whatever it sees. Think of the "instant nostalgia" of Restoration Hardware. Who else is noticing these things as the unpurged images of the Matrix recede?

Beck does it for me. Many will find him rather hard on the ear, but given the media saturation and all-at-onceness of our historical moment, let me urge that the apparent distortion associated with his work is not only permissible but necessary. In the era of the bombarded soul, the artist will often do well to bombard back. And Beck, as a student of Smith's *Anthology*, asks how the old troubadours might respond to our time. He suspects they'd be a deeply disturbed bunch, and getting the good word out to the people would take some doing. Outlandish times call for some outlandish measures. While his music is perfectly capable of presenting itself in a guitar/harmonica format (as he demonstrates in his mostly acoustic *One Foot in the Grave*), Beck also understands that acquiring and maintaining an audience will require a block-rocking beat or two. This isn't to say he's stooping, because his appreciation of multiple genres of music is wide-ranging and often appears encyclopedic. He takes as a given the presence of his beloved protest-folk sensiblity in that which is categorized as Hip Hop, the same bravado and boastful, nonsense storytelling of a semifictional persona who will drink his coffee from a hubcap and "swing through the city on a wreckin' ball" with "plastic on my mind."

What to do with all the wreckage? Is there anything or anyplace that might still bear the name of life? Ever one to remind us of the apocalyptic purposes of the poet, Marshall McLuhan provides us with a wonderful illustration in the creative processes of William Butler Yeats:

> In recounting the making of "The Lake Isle of Innisfree," Yeats tells how he was contemplating an advertisement for soft drinks in a London shop window where a tiny ball was dancing on top of a jet of water to convey the sportive, emancipated quality of the beverage. While Yeats stood on the pavement in the eye-, ear-, and air-polluted metropolis, he proceeded to create an anti-environment, namely "innisfree," in order to make sense of the anarchy of the world around him.[1]

Imagining Yeats staring dumbfounded at a soft drink advertisement, composing a word of resistance in his head, is perhaps the best way to begin our consideration of the importance of being Beck. Art as a counterenvironment (and here, we may think of the forces of Zion in *The Matrix* as well as the subversive imagination of Radiohead) will involve embrace as well as renunciation, and Beck roams the aftermath in search of abandoned cliches, rejected fragments, and discarded images that might serve as burning embers. Gazing upon a dead, out-of-date world that once looked so new, maybe we can make the dry bones dance, breathing upon the ancient (and newly) slain that they may live.

While many songwriters make their living by taking everyday sayings and copying them directly into the chorus of a radio single, Beck invents his own sayings (loosely composed of old ones) appropriate to the madness of the age. He will use any means at his disposal to name, mock, and rearrange the dissembling spirits of our day and render them ridiculous by giving the forces of darkness such titles as "stereopathetic soul manure" and "a bozo nightmare." His lyrics reflect a perpetual apprehension that refuses to be paralyzed or silenced and, instead, employs mockery and outlandish imagery as a form of hopeful protest. On the anthems of *Mellow Gold*, the party summons of *Odelay*, the haunted world of *Mutations*, and the mad, comic nightmare of *Midnite Vultures*, we're persuaded to look twice at our own troubled, groaning terrain. In a world of media saturation that transforms human affection into something groping and soulless, Beck's swiftly evolving metaphors refuse submission to the manipulative orchestrations of a death-dealing culture and form an overall pattern of alternative clarity and mindfulness against disharmony and fear.

"The Power of the Air"

In his first major release, *Mellow Gold*, Beck's one indisputable radio smash, "Loser," provides us with the cautionary motto that we mustn't believe everything that we breathe, a theme that informs most of his work thus far. As is typical of a Beck song, it's an emancipation proclamation embedded among numerous haphazard images that reveal and connect themselves with every new listen. It's as if he crams in as many phrases as the ear can take and far too many to get it all in one go. In "Loser," the psychology of self-delusion is made apparent when, over the sound of blues guitar licks, drum beats, and a sitar, we hear the sample of a voice confidently declaring itself "a winner" and declaring that changes are in the air. Such feverishly held confidence is countered in "Painted Eyelids," which senses limitless limitations floating in the air.

Death and delusion in the air and the vulnerability of the mind to dehumanizing forces will persist throughout Beck's work. Alongside Morpheus's tutorial taunt to Neo ("Do you think that's air you're breathing now?"), we can add the oddly Beck-like observation of Walter Wink who describes the "power of the air" of Ephesians 2:2 as "the spiritual matrix of inauthentic living" that wins our "unwitting obedience" as a "pseudo-environment that ascribes to itself absoluteness and permanence," having been "created by the sum total of choices for evil." It is what we might call Old Mechanical or "the way of the world." Wink puts the matter powerfully:

> It is, in short, what we mean today by such terms as ideologies, the Zeitgeist, customs, public opinion, peer pressure, institutional expectations, mob psychology, jingoistic patriotism, and negative vibes. These constitute the "power of the air," the invisible but palpable environment of opinions, beliefs, propaganda, convictions, prejudices, hatreds, racial and class biases, taboos, and loyalties that condition our perception of the world long before we reach the age of choice, often before we reach the age of speech. It "kills" us precisely because we breathe it in before we even realize it is noxious. Like fish in water, we are not even aware that it exists, much less that it determines the way we think, speak, and act.[2]

Apocalyptic exposes "it" wherever the desensitizing madness lurks. We mustn't tire of trying out language to name these antagonistic powers. Like Yeats in front of the media onslaught, we will occasionally have to pull out the poetry. I believe my wife inadvertently expresses such apocalyptic insight when she says of a conversation, a meeting, or an event, "The electricity was all wrong."

Beck's "Whiskeyclone, Hotel City 1997" describes the feeling of futility in even trying to think these matters through when everything we're learning is wrong. And lest we bluff ourselves into thinking a rock and roll lifestyle has set us free, the aptly-titled "Pay No Mind," suggests that, on our way past the morgues, the overflowing toilets, and the shopping malls emerging out of the walls, we do well to offer "the finger to the rock and roll singer" who dances on our paychecks.

Most performers deny themselves (and their audiences) such subversive insights, but Beck seems interested in little else. "Soul Suckin Jerk," gives a voice to millions of fast-food workers the world over who make money for the man by tossing "chicken in the bucket with the soda pop can." The protagonist of the song will give the finger to the "power of the air" by stripping off his "puke green uniform" and setting it on fire "in a vat of chicken fat." After running through the mini-mall half-naked, the newly emancipated, ex-employee has momentarily broken free from all things "Soul Suckin," but his liberty doesn't bring much in the way of fulfillment as he stands with a beer in his hand and a mouth full of sand. A similarly tragicomic plight faces the protagonist of "Mexico," who has lost his job at McDonalds after being too scared to call the police immediately following a robbery. In an effort at self-assertion and vengeance, he conspires with some friends to rob the McDonalds himself to fund a raucous weekend in Mexico. They succeed, but after a drunken binge, his friends abandon him and he soon assumes a position at another McDonalds in Mexico.

Beck's keeping it real with whatever poetic phrases best capture this malaise. Oftentimes they're too ridiculous and painful to entertain for long. There is an "unwitting obedience" that finds it all too nonsensical to bother with, but the cathartic quality of Beck's undomesticated expressions is a life-giving spirit. It is the enemy of all that numbs.

101

Tired Old Asylum

Before moving on to the Grammy-winning *Odelay*, it might be helpful to note Beck's understanding of what we might call negative capability and the moral necessity of leaving well enough alone. His work walks a kind of tightrope between the twin dangers of an apathetic cynicism and the totalizing gaze that murders to dissect. To the best of his ability, Beck tries to represent the more true (and therefore more difficult) way of embrace.

Beck is well acquainted with his culture's fear of being caught embracing something, but he's unwilling to accept this understandable anxiety as an excuse. It leads inevitably to using disappointment as a lifestyle and an available excuse for inaction. His mostly ignored ballad, "Feather In Your Cap," confronts this fear in an uncharacteristically direct fashion, telling the listener to "make a move" with whatever is at hand even as "dead waters" rise above our powers of comprehension. Again, the apocalyptic imagination understands that we can't embrace that which we claim to wholly understand, and Beck notes the dangers in wanting the truth "so you can crush it in your hand." Crushing the paradoxical is the way of death, and being moved and humbled before the enigmatic everyday is the life-affirming alternative. Explaining it away or casting it aside is an Enlightenment lunacy. The song continues with the assertion that the absence of a map for the journey need not leave us tangled or tired. There are worse mental states than being uncertain, and viewing truth as either a possession or easily crushed nonsense can leave us singing to ourselves in a "tired old asylum." This is a Swiftian contempt for both the fanaticism that claims to know all things and the apathy that self-righteously refuses to know anything.

In living out this path, Beck is determined to recognize and unveil the beauty of discarded objects from green-glass bottles to Campbell's soup cans. His unwillingness to let any epiphany go unnoticed has me wondering and expectant over what kind of work he'll do if he ever has a child. We can know that his language will body forth something other than a cliche-ridden sentimentality.

Beck understands that faithfully learning from the ancient wisdom of the past will require fresh articulations of what's come before. He can't settle for the worn out coinage of yesterday's wineskins. As he explains in an interview with *Rolling Stone*, this is the peculiar burden of his generation:

> My whole generation's mission is to kill the cliche. I don't know whether it's conscious all the time, but it's one of the reasons a lot of my generation is always on the fence about things. They're afraid to commit to anything for fear of seeming like a cliche. They're afraid to commit to their lives because they see so much of the world as a cliche. So I'm trying to embrace the world and all this stuff in a way that doesn't seem cliche. I'm creating the new cliche.[3]

Interesting to note that he leaves it to future generations to render the verdict concerning his own work and whether it's a classic, for all time, or another cliche with limited shelf-life. An unwillingness to judge oneself or to think too self-consciously about one's relevance in the present or in the context of history distinguishes Beck from the general neuroses of celebrity culture. He understands that such shameful self-conscious thinking is a "tired old asylum" with no exit, and instead seeks to practice the wisdom that knows there are worse fates than not gaining "the world."

As the satirists of the past understood, this practice is a full-time vocation that can't be undertaken without hilarity. There will be slip-ups and false starts, as the "New Pollution" is, as we should know by now, everywhere. But an eternally amused sympathy is, hopefully, also at work. One of O'Connor's favorites, Georges Bernanos, offers a description of the cosmic context of a grand sympathy which, I like to think, would make Beck smile:

> The fool who constructs theories and makes judgments may still move the Angels to pity. He is practicing his unreason within the space of God's mercy, as a baby relieves itself in its diapers. By contrast, when a cynical brute whips his fury into ecstasy and is panting from his exertion to enter into the great All, then heaven and earth are dismayed.[4]

The Mind Is Its Own Place

A good four hundred years before Beck put pen to paper, John Donne looked at his world of scientific revolution and related religious upheaval and declared, " 'Tis all in pieces, all coherence gone." In an effort to explain the present phenomenon to itself, he employed the language of numerous disciplines (science, philosophy, religion) in what would come to be called metaphysical poetry. Such poetry is marked by the presence of the metaphysical conceit, which bends logic by linking together objects and ideas in a mixture that breaks the normal rules of association. This was the only way Donne could hope to truthfully chronicle his moment. Even now, Donne's meaning will often strike us at times as unnecessarily obtuse. We can imagine the difficulty his work would present if he'd lived in the age of television and shopping malls.

As Donne taunts the occupying forces of evil ("Death, thou shalt die"), no imagery is too far-fetched or too humiliatingly personal. In Holy Sonnet 14, for instance, he confesses that not only has he engaged himself to Satan but he's personally thwarted, repeatedly, the attempts of his "three-personed God" to divorce him from this debilitating relationship. He keeps going back to the Prince of Darkness, because he (Donne) is an accomplice in his own destruction, not a victim. His imagination has been colonized, and only a battering can break the siege. Only a ravishing will purify him. Such paradoxes are essential to apocalyptic expression. They dislocate the mind toward new awareness. It's in the necessarily disconcerting context of metaphysical poetry that we might best understand Beck's confession of a consciousness fading in and out at an alarming rate, dead-ends around every corner, "briefcase blues," and the insistent realization/confession that he possesses "a devil's haircut" in his mind.

This is the opening track of *Odelay*. Musically, it's an incredibly lively beginning that urges its subject matter upon the listener in a powerfully subversive fashion. For those with a taste for the loud and raucous, it's as if we're nodding approvingly before we know exactly what we're agreeing to, what morally deficient state we're confessing to be our own. As ever, a complete take on every image would mean a treatment of each line of the song, but the final verse suggests that the very medium of rock and roll is a questionable (and possibly deceptive) means for transmitting his meaning as his sanity ghetto blasts itself into nothing.

The surrounding disintegration and expanding emptiness in the atmosphere are walk-on characters, in some fashion, in every Beck song, and he never tires of shining a light on whatever demonic manifestations are lurking in the shadows. But the investigative aspect of his wordplay is also determined, while gazing into the abyss, to ask what yet in this might still be fit for redemption. When life is spotted, his job is to lift it up, however mundane it might initially appear, in a celebratory gesture.

But this can't be done without looking hard at the paradoxical within the everyday, paying attention to overheard conversations and background noises, and making the necessary connections. The apocalyptic mind will view every moment as a possible revelation. "Lord Only Knows" warns of the wasted opportunity involved when we take for granted "what the Lord's laid on the floor." Beck, however, is not so proud as he picks up the pieces and puts them up for sale. The given, after all, is what we'll either use and view well or miss all together. Beck advocates embracing it as a possible sacrament. How else do we expect to find and facilitate the grace-ridden poetry of everyday? The least we can do is notice. Otherwise, the festivities of renovation and transformation will happen without us.

"A Strange Invitation"

While it will no doubt constitute a wide-awakeness to which we're mostly unaccustomed, the life-affirming business of practicing a fascinated affection within the machine is the only alternative, even as it brings with it the realization that we're often powered by something other than soul. Putting the soul back in demands spotting it in all sorts of unlikely places and allowing the possibility that whatever we're currently considering our good moments aren't actually good enough. Without these allowances, we're stuck. We need something to push us forward; something to keep us from being settled, finished, and done in the confines of made-up minds. Who will save us from the impending dead-ends and invite us to lay hold of more than cool reason ever comprehends?

Finally comes the poet, that unacknowledged legislator of worlds. I don't know if Beck has Shakespeare in mind in "Where It's At" when he intones, over a revelatory organ and drumbeat, that we'll find "a destination a little up the road" just past "the habitations and the towns we know" where the lights are less blinding and we're blessed with the sound of "jig-saw jazz," but I wouldn't be surprised. It certainly puts me in the mind of *A Midsummer Night's Dream*, in which Theseus describes the poetic eye "in a fine frenzy rolling," and imagination bodying forth "the form of things unknown," transforming them into shapes and giving "to aery nothing a local habitation and a name." Beck's admonition to pick ourselves up off the side of the road and give ourselves a call is certainly a summons to imagine differently, to enter a kind of performance poetry that will invigorate and strengthen against the "hypnotizers" on hand. It's the job of the poet to take us somewhere further up the road, somewhere we're currently not. And while he never invites the trees of the field to clap their hands or the rocks to cry out, he does put the readily available to a brave new use as he commands the "bottles and cans" to clap their hands. As ever, he's picking up the pieces of the old world (all that the Lord's laid on the floor) and hammering together a new one of greater constancy.

Odelay finally lands in something of a foul rag-and-bone shop of the heart. The beautiful dirge that is "Ramshackle" offers a tired hopefulness in the uncertainty of destination. The ghost town imagery presented in this rite of passage provokes thoughts of parting with one's belongings, tightly-held ambitions, and all the things to which we cling unkindly. It's as if all the living must wind down and stick together before it will be accorded the privileges of motion, before deadweight is fit for resurrection. The clenched fist has to surrender to the open hand.

Plague of Phantoms

Slowing down long enough to see clearly will often feel like a more strenuous feat than keeping up with the rat race. Sometimes silence only affords unbidden words and images the opportunity to spring up and take hold. On the subject of overly specific and needlessly graphic recollection, Petrarch offers this description:

> The innumerable forms and images of visible things, let in one after the other, gather together and pile up at the bottom of the soul. . . . They weigh it down and worry it; the soul isn't made for this; it can't hold so many deformed objects. From this springs that plague of phantoms who dissipate our thoughts and whose pernicious variety bars the way to luminous contemplation.[5]

While a good many singer/songwriters frequently concern themselves specifically with the confusion of our age, no performer I know of is as weighed down as Beck on the subject of the worried, saturated soul that only knows how to sell itself short. It's as if he's stepped out of a time machine, studied the surrounding Western culture, and taken it upon himself to make known the hideous abnormalities that disguise themselves as natural, to expose the pretentious sentiments that only feign benevolence. This is a work of scathing criticism that is nevertheless born of hope, a hope that insists that surely this isn't the best we can do while pointing to a destination a little up the road. Keep looking. We weren't made for these self-inflicted horrors.

If *Odelay* outlined the madness with humor and hope, *Mutations* is almost exclusively an imaginatively worded lamentation. By skillfully describing a culture whose passions are ridiculous and soulless, it somehow clears the air for some luminous contemplation. Of course, it does afford a few laughs, but this time around you can't exactly call his kaleidoscopic stream of metaphors an exaggeration (as is certainly the case with *Midnite Vultures*). To say that in recent history human behavior and self-understanding have undergone a number of mutations and that the indignities of the present exceed anything our hypothetical time-traveler might have anticipated is to state the obvious. *Mutations* offers an apocalyptic sketch of the reigning phantoms, a journal of the plague with terminology from many eras and multiple genres. File under "Sci-fi Folk."

107

We are a generation disowned and "corroded to the bone." This is Beck's diagnosis of our new world order in "Cold Brains." Importantly, we should note the first-person plural. There is no condescension or self-exemption from the cold, unmoved, untouched consciences that distinguish us from our ancestors. It should come as no surprise when our conversations and attempted interactions ring devastatingly hollow along our "trail of disasters." No moralizing.

"Cancelled Check" gives us a bit of comic relief without relinquishing the weight of moral bankruptcy throughout the album. Beck explained to National Public Radio that inspiration for the song came from an infomercial in which a motivational speaker announced "The past is a cancelled check, your maximum point of power is now!" The emptiness and delusional power of such slogans are only partially reduced by their transparent opportunism that offers nothing more than "a rotten egg." Hunting down "the maximum point of power" is unveiled as the broad path that leads to destruction.

This is the engine of madness, delivering dreams absurd, hideous, and pitiful. "We Live Again" is a confessional hymn of "withered hands" that dig for dreams in the refuse of "leftover nightmares." It continues the naming of an all-corrupting evil, an idiot wind that "blows my soul crazy." Discerning its presence is a difficult undertaking in a "newfangled wasteland," but there's a glimmer of hope for the young whose wildernesses will burn in a day of love made new and nevermore "cold and vacant."

Static

Given Beck's ongoing shock, early in his career, when his music was most loudly appreciated by the very people whose lifestyles are the targets of his art, it might be a safe bet to view "Tropicalia" as a kind of self-assessment concerning the place the young singer has found himself—"singing funeral songs" to the "anabolic and bronze" who eventually "fall down and deflate." While he can commend an alternative mode of viewing the world by way of his extravagant presentation, his enthusiasm for the downtrodden and discarded is ultimately a kind of poverty that, by its nature, will not last long on the musical charts or sell too many units. Life beneath "an air-conditioned sun" might please the eyes momentarily, but never the heart.

This is a fairly devastating critique of his own generation's cultural moment. The commentary continues with "Bottle of Blues" where he's holding hands with impotent delusions in brothels of fake energy while being pounded by "crippled psalms of an age that won't thaw." The brothel will receive its most extensive treatment on *Midnite Vultures*. Till then, the wasted sentiments proliferate and on "O Maria," Beck points out the self-deception is perhaps only skin deep as most sense the fabric of folly falling apart around us. And like the proverbial frog in water gradually brought to a boil, death will creep in slow while inspiring a sense of safety. He'll go much much further, but the "death" he names here (which peeks behind the curtain throughout *Mutations*) might be considered Beck's primary preoccupation. It could be said to inform, in some fashion, every song he's ever put out. This "power of the air" or "static" is a force of seemingly endless brightness, thick with long established and still-to-come stratagems, as ever-present as oxygen, and hell-bent on nothing less specific than the gradual deformation and eventual destruction of your soul. In the meantime, as O'Connor's Misfit assures us, "the pleasures are seldom and few."

Cavalry Drums

As we wonder what sort of landscape Beck is tackling on *Midnite Vultures*, we might go to the trouble of noting the kind of situation vultures are known to favor and conclude that he is offering us an unconventional take on the romanticized, mythic culture of midnite (spelled party-style). He's already illustrated the spirits that solicit affection, advertise it, and never deliver. They subliminally instruct "insert soul here" and leave the client empty. Advertising technology is calibrated to incite, after all, and it isn't doing its job if it doesn't. While this principle describes the straightforward, supposedly innocuous methods of commercialization,

Beck will unmask the ways in which this corrupting influence has made its way into interpersonal relationships while wondering out loud if anyone knows the difference anymore. He wants to disabuse us of these false dreams through a comedic sleaze vision.

Beck knows that he's trafficking in the stuff of nightmare fantasy, and *Midnite Vultures* will concern itself primarily with the natural outcome of *libido dominandi*, a worldview whose only discernible motive is "the pursuit of happiness." In the tradition of Jonathan Swift, this is Beck's "Modest Proposal." We're treated to the horrors of possessive individualism. He will not dignify the sexuality described in "Sexx Laws" with a proper spelling, and the album opens with a storm warning concerning the aforementioned static-like force that now assumes the form of an attacking army whose cavalry drums announce the hijacking of our equilibriums. Haven't you come to realize that your peace of mind (if you had any to begin with) is being taken over by hostile forces? In each verse, he describes our current state of affairs, which includes perfumed men acting like concubines, pixilated doctors moaning, and it always leads up to the chorus which serves as a kind of mission statement announcing a resolute defiance against the twisted logic of sexx laws. When pressed in an interview, Beck remarks that this refers to his personal determination to overcome the expectations of his social milieu. If the madness of the age defines the way things have to be, he'll have none of it. Let the handcuffs be loosed, and we'll accompany one another in the halfway homes of recovery. Beck will not be cowed by the cavalry. He is "a full-grown man" who's "not afraid to cry." If the inclination to weep and mourn had been professed on a slow, acoustic *Mutations*-style track, we'd detect his tone easily enough. As it is, he's jazzed up the crippled psalm (a cry of protest) and picked up the pace by giving it the feel of a game show theme song.

In his previous work, one can easily view Beck's attempts at poetic wisdom, asking what form it might assume in these troubled days. He exhibits the old respect and reluctance that delays judgment and examines the vessel before getting on board. Willing to wait for the next one if necessary. No hurry. But on *Midnite Vultures*, he's doing something a little more complicated. He's describing a sinking ship on fire and giving a voice to any number of its passengers interchangeably. He suggests in interviews that it's a party record that, when listened to attentively, might not be the kind of party anyone would actually want to attend. These are images that, when rightly gazed upon, will depict the multiplying villainies of nature swarming upon us.

"Nicotine & Gravy," offers a world which inverts the inheritance of a land flowing with milk and honey and somehow channels an ancient Egyptian landscape along with the plagues heaped upon it for its stubbornness. Surviving at all is a miracle in this environment, where fear and lunacy fund the economy. The sense that we're going crazy in the throes of a living death of soul massage pervades the atmosphere, and "the poignant rain" goes unacknowledged as we further busy ourselves with slumber.

Beck is naming the mostly unnamed evils of middle-class culture with such precision that he should receive an award from whatever organizations concern themselves with "family issues" or "eternal values" in media. "Mixed Bizness" features lunatics reaching for eye drops so they can keep their eyes open to better see the dancing girls in a slaughterhouse of the spirit. "Get Real Paid" scrutinizes and laments the widespread separation of sexual activity and genuine affection by asking how it feels to be covered like butter and left in the gutter. And "Hollywood Freaks" notes that those who could serve as shamans, restoring clarity and vision, have gone cripple and settle for tripled sales with their "lobotomy beats." It goes on to offer a panoply of horrific scenarios while repeatedly asking if we *really* want to feel this.

"Peaches & Cream" is a satirical ode to the practice of blissful ignorance in what we call, without even pretending to mean it, "love." With a gently weeping guitar, it begins with the ironically applied biblical principle to not let your right hand know what your left hand is doing. This sexual propositioning is prefaced with the less-than-convincing assurance that the predator will "let you down easy" and that it's all just a dream. This is Beck's deeply moral response to a world gone wrong. If all of this isn't obvious enough, he connects the dots for us with the insertion of a chorus at the end offering the advice, given to the bridesmaids in Jesus' parable about the coming kingdom of God, to keep our lamplights trimmed and burning.

But such references shouldn't shock us too much on an album constantly declaring that we're all "out of control" and that none of us know "how low we'll go." Beck isn't the only voice suggesting that we're inhabiting "a garden of sleaze," but he's one of the few who manages to say as much while keeping the room dancing. He chronicles how death has undone so many while pointing forward to "someone calling your name" while a hurricane is blowing your way.

We know the deal.

Perhaps the classic ballad that best characterizes the album is the brutally funny, powerfully falsetto "Debra." It could easily be considered Beck's very own "To His Coy Mistress." The apparent sincerity of the pseudo-suitor distracts the listener from the immodesty of his proposal. As he recounts his acquaintance with his object of desire thus far, he notes that he met her in a JC Penney and that he *thinks* her nametag said "Jenny." When we note the title *and* the uncertainty with which our young man recalls the girl's name, it's clear that something is up. The worst is yet to come. "You've got a thing," he observes, and the "thing" is something that he has "got to get with." And, if it could be arranged, he'd like to include her sister in the arrangement. He thinks her name is Debra.

In terms of unmasking folly, this might not seem like much. But when we observe all the imagery and language that passes unquestioned under the radar advertised in the guise of love and romance, there's a comedic subversiveness here that's downright scathing. The protagonist goes on to promise a ride in his Hyundai and "a real good meal." And the subtle inhumanities for which we settle comes through in his casual observance of a standard procedure. There's really no point in wasting time "gettin' to know each other," because she knows "the deal."

Admittedly, this is satire, but it's also a deeply insightful illustration of the ins and outs of what it might serve us well to term consensual sexual abuse. Both REM and U2 have explored this mutually-agreed-upon territory of madness, but only rarely to such hilarious effect. If we knew for certain that the fellow actually

112

knew either woman's name, we might accept his claim that he has "a little bit of sympathy" for her. But by the end of it, the strange invader's repeated refrain that she drives him "crazy" is, by all criteria, completely truthful nightmare stuff. Beck has single-handedly destroyed and helpfully redefined, in a morally illuminating way, this particular cliche of the so-called "love" song.

Beck is very clearly awake. To my knowledge, there's almost no one fulfilling the particular apocalyptic function he's carved out for himself. In the multifaceted imagery that assaults on a constant basis, he looks (often in vain) for the motive that's more than merely fleshly, more than units sold and money made. He's looking for the soul. When he expresses his findings, instead of simply reflecting them, they are necessarily disjointed. And the disjointed poetry expresses, metaphysically, the ways in which we go about embezzling our own souls. Beck reminds us that this error is bred in the bone, and that we've grown so accustomed to wasting our affections on the synthetic and the artificial that the presence of real people and the possibility of authentic interaction strikes us as discomforting and unacceptable. While the imagery of technology appears to know no boundaries in its ongoing exploitation, we should pause long enough to acknowledge that we don't know fully how it works. We don't know what it is, exactly, that it does to us or in what strange ways its driven us to look at one another. Like few voices currently on the air, Beck calls our attention to the incomprehensible damage we've undergone and inflicted. Ironically, all that many music reviewers can think to say concerning Beck is that he's eclectic.

The darkened mind, incapable of (or no longer interested in) struggling with itself, will find little of interest in Beck. But there is plenty to illumine what is dark within us when we open ourselves to the waiting, wide-awake day and its blessedly paradoxical inhabitants. Slipping behind the rationalizations of "progress," Beck measures its painstakingly orchestrated *and* categorically denied "impact," and represents on behalf of the casualties with their casual frowns. Like a postmodern pilgrim raising a voice in the wake of sightless visions, Beck exemplifies a receptive, complex moral imagination whose poetry will, if we're attentive, give to aery nothing a local habitation and a name.

SEVEN

Daylight Is a Dream If You've Lived with Your Eyes Closed

The Cinematic Epiphanies of Joel and Ethan Coen

The rational gaze on space evaporates the real into phantoms, whereas to hold on to each reality we must regard it as an unfathomable "revelation."

John Milbank, *Radical Orthodoxy*

The trouble with folks like Brownie is they hold their life in like a bakebean fart at a Baptist cookout and only let it slip out sideways a little at a time when they think there's nobody noticing. Now that's the last thing on earth the Almighty intended. He intended all the

114

life a man's got inside him, he should live it out just as free and strong and natural as a bird.

Leo Bebb in Frederick Buechner's *Treasure Hunt*

As a teenager, I emerged from my first viewing of *Raising Arizona* feeling certain that, within the space of two hours, my universe had been undone and put back together again. There was nothing especially unfamiliar about the world that had passed before me—the sayings and verbal quips of the characters, their mannerisms, their rage, and the advertising language and folk wisdom with which they tried to make sense of their lives. But my own world, the one in which all this hilarious beauty had been going on around me all along, was made new.

Raising Arizona became a standard by which all other artistic expression, in my arrogant young mind, would be measured. If it didn't have that ineffably true take on reality, the transcendent weirdness of this vision, what was the point? And how should I feel about the viewer who doesn't (or can't) get it? I found myself mercilessly judging anyone who only found *Raising Arizona* "interesting." To resist its glories was to resist the enigmatic music of life itself.

It took my tutelage at the hands of Flannery O'Connor, among others, to begin to liberate me from this bondage of death, seeking to extract the mote of fastidiousness in my neighbor's eye while blinded by the lumber in my own. Being shocked free of this snobbery is, I suppose, an ongoing process. I still maintain, however, that the films of Joel and Ethan Coen assist in this very process of deliverance. Like nobody I can think of, they've taken up O'Connor's mantle of depicting and dignifying the grotesque. And like O'Connor, they're often charged with perhaps enjoying the murderous messes their characters get into a little too much. But following her lead, they call it like they see it. Predictably enough, what they see is blood red revelation.

Well-intentioned sugar-coating is clearly a disaster—the opposite of respect, in fact. *Fargo*, for instance, opens with an amused but deeply insightful taunt (completely fabricated by the way) to their squeamish despisers: "This is a true story. The events depicted

115

in this film took place in Minnesota in 1987. At the request of the survivors, the names have been changed. Out of respect for the dead, the rest has been told exactly as it occurred." The truthfully rendered story will look hard at humiliation *and* heroism, and neither unambiguously. It's a matter of respect. Nothing is good without it.

As a Coen film ends, I have the distinct pleasure of knowing I've seen something good without knowing exactly why. O'Connor tells us that if artistic expression is to be wholesome, it will have to start by being whole, and every Coen film is embarrassingly whole. They give us the whole of whatever story they're telling. From the child stealing the toupee of a dead mobster (with a dog watching him do it) to the car buyer summoning the nerve to use an expletive against a duplicitous salesman to the coffee ring circling the newspaper's one feasible job description to a hotel clerk repeating himself, this overflowing abundance and the maddening attention to detail put other films (and most novels) to shame. As it always is with the wholesome, the meanings are ever dawning. They come to us over time as phrases, scenes, and images collide and caress and impact our minds. This is the characteristic effect of apocalyptic.

That Barton Fink Feeling

The beauty-drenched grandeur afforded by paying close attention to the unfathomable revelation that is the surrounding world is the artist's special inheritance. It is this inheritance that bombards John Tuturro's playwright Barton Fink from every angle and against which he maintains an invincible ignorance. He is too convinced of his own empathic and earth-shatteringly effective love for "the common man" ("I guess I try to make a difference"), and he's too in love with his own bad poetry, which describes, for instance, a train going by "like a cast-iron wind," and proclaims what will prove to be such self-inflictedly prophetic gems as "Daylight is a dream when you've lived with your eyes closed." His manager, Garland, suggests that a Hollywood writing job might not be completely irrelevant to his humanitarian aspirations: "The com-

116

mon man'll still be here when you get back. What the hell, they might even have one or two of 'em out in Hollywood." His knee-jerk response: "That's a rationalization, Garland." Garland: "Barton, it was a joke." Such jokes might let in a little air as the roaring wave of reality crashes on the shore, but as is his habit, Barton isn't paying attention.

The entire film, in fact, is filled with little serendipitous insights that, like burning coals, might potentially poke through the hopeless closed-uppedness of Barton's "life of the mind." Every character unwittingly speaks to his failure but none more outrageously than John Goodman's Charlie Meadows. As Barton sits in his hotel room dimly staring at a painting of a woman on a beach above his typewriter, the sound of an ocean wave that accompanies many an epiphanic occasion gradually turns to the laughter and weeping of his neighbor next door. He's expounded long and proudly about the audibility of such sounds, but as it's coming at him, he's only annoyed by it. He doesn't actually *want* to hear the cry of "the common man."

Having telephoned Chet with his complaint, Barton waits with a sense of horror as he overhears the neighbor, Charlie, receiving the call from downstairs to quiet down and making his way over to Barton's room. As Charlie offers him a drink by way of apology, the conversation that ensues is vintage Coen brothers. It is the stuff of highest comedy.

Charlie's insurance business is, in his words, a work of "human contact." He good-naturedly assumes that this might be of interest to him as Barton declares, "The hopes and dreams of the common man are as noble as those of any king. It's the stuff of life—why shouldn't it be the stuff of theater?" Since Barton's job is the chronicling of the human spirit, Charlie begins his repeated offer, "I could tell you some stories—." But Barton is too enamored with his own words to acknowledge the word made flesh sitting beside him. "I could tell you some stories—," Charlie begins. Barton cuts him off:

Sure you could! And yet many writers do everything in their power to insulate themselves from the common man—from where they live, from where they trade, from where they fight and love and converse and—and—and . . . so naturally their work suffers, and regresses into empty formalism and—well, I'm spouting off again, but to put it in your language, the theater becomes as phony as a three-dollar bill.

"Yeah, I guess that's tragedy right there," Charlie notes. And Barton's response (which didn't make the final cut), utterly oblivious to any self-application, might have been one of the most succinct statements of solipsism ever spoken in cinema: "Frequently played, seldom remarked." Charlie laughs knowingly and adds, "Whatever that means."

With his toweringly mad wit, Charlie, the common man, is running circles around Barton. He is perversely aware of the role Barton wants him to play, and he cannot resist inserting little hints and jabs concerning Barton's cluelessness and moral failure into his colloquialisms. While Barton assumes that its his responsibility to express himself in language the likes of Charlie might understand, Charlie is composing poetry into his ear. The mysteries of the human are beyond Barton and the viewer. We have no idea what we're seeing when we look into a human face, and we do measureless damage when we think we do. Charlie, we will find out, is a psycho killer.

Barton smiles condescendingly and apologizes for boring him. Charlie's mockery continues: "No! . . . I'm the kind of guy, I'll let you know if I'm bored. I find it all pretty d—ned interesting. I'm the kind of schmoe who's generally interested in the other guy's point of view." Barton plays into Charlie's improvisation perfectly: "Well, we've got something in common then." Can he be of any help to him, he asks. "Sure, sure Charlie, you can help by just being yourself." After offering again to give him a story or two, Charlie apologizes once more for the interruption and throws out a poignant parting taunt: "Too much revelry late at night, you forget there are other people in the world."

This forgetfulness and failure of the imagination is what we may call, using the language of the film, "that Barton Fink feeling." It's the opposite of Tom Reagan's steely dictum in *Miller's Crossing*: "Nobody knows anybody." It's the delusion, void of any real empathy, that calls itself an artistic impulse. It's what Capitol

Pictures' Jack Lipnick mistakenly assumes is Barton's genuine prophetic inspiration:

> We're only interested in one thing: Can you tell a story, Bart? Can you make us laugh, can you make us cry, can you make us wanna break out in joyous song? Is that more than one thing? The important thing is we all have that Barton Fink feeling, but since you're Barton Fink I'm assuming you have it in spades.

Lipnick is only partly right. We do, all of us, have the Barton Fink feeling, but it isn't the celestial power of self-forgetting imagination. It's the epidemic overestimation of our own ability to understand ourselves, the people around us, and the sweet old world. It's the tendency to view the world through the lens of our own vanity. As we're shown in almost every Coen film, the Barton Fink feeling is a killer. And sometimes I think it is the prophetic vocation of Ethan and Joel Coen to disabuse their public of this destructive force by any means necessary. This is a deeply moral work, particularly well-exemplified by Flannery O'Connor, and it will be especially misunderstood by those minds most maddeningly possessed by the Barton Fink feeling.

We might say that one story of an artist's liberation from such ignorant pride can be found in Preston Sturges's *Sullivan's Travels*. Like Barton, film director Sullivan has a pretension or two in the direction of what his work, *O Brother Where Art Thou?* will accomplish, and in language reminiscent of Lipnick's hopes for Barton he can barely contain himself: *"O Brother Where Art Thou? is going to be the greatest tragedy ever made. The world will weep, humanity will sob."* Over time, Sullivan recovers from his delusions and settles on a principle that serves the Coens well: "There's a lot to be said for making people laugh. That's all they've got in this cock-eyed caravan." Barton's waking-up process will have a few more casualties, but the cruel wisdom descending upon him will not be without laughter. As the student of apocalyptic understands, the murdering, laughable, folly-ridden inclinations of the human heart will not accommodate themselves to our categories. Trying to make them do so is a blurring of vision and a perversion of truthfulness. Despite the good intentions of such perversions, the Coens will have none of it.

Little Entertainments

In stark contrast to Barton's self-conscious and ineffectual "great inner pain," we have a walk-in part for William Faulkner in the thinly disguised W. P. Mayhew. "Ain't writin' peace?" he asks as he gazes up at the trees and takes in the air. Mayhew writes to escape, and the effortlessness with which he delivers the goods on his apocalyptic vocation is brought home with the thud of his latest novel *Nebuchadnezzar* dropped in front of Barton. Its inscription: "To Barton—May this little entertainment divert you in your sojourn among the Philistines."

Mayhew's peace, however, comes to him between bouts of alcohol-drenched depression. The stakes of speaking truth to power, of accurately giving meaning to their hopes and fears, are evident in the passage from the Book of Daniel upon which Barton happens in his hotel room:

> And the king, Nebuchadnezzar, answered and said to the Chaldeans, I recall not my dream; if ye will not make known unto me my dream, and its interpretation, ye shall be cut in pieces, and of your tents shall be made a dunghill.

His ongoing, God-given job is the dream made known, and as Mayhew attests in his drunken stupor, it's the job or the dunghill: "I'm buildin' a levee. Gulp by gulp, brick by brick. Raisin' up a levee to keep that ragin' river of manure from lappin' at m'door."

As Mayhew appears to understand, this is certainly Barton's calling as well. But Barton's anguished response to the call, in Mayhew's view, is a sign of his dimwittedness:

"Mmm. Wal, me, I just enjoy makin' things up." This is the "little entertainment" which, according to Mayhew, O'Connor, and the Coens, is all any of us can manage. We interpret the dream by entertaining what's actually there in a sweet unrest, in a humbled awe, not by constipated concentration. As Mayhew puts it, "The truth, m'honey, is a tart that does not bear scrutiny." When Mayhew's mistress, Audrey, tries to explain to Barton that empathy requires understanding, all he can do is ask rhetorically, "What don't I understand?"

Alone in his room, Barton slaves away at nothing with the heat building up and the occasional glance at the woman in the picture above him. After his failed vocation has brought murderous destruction and his career is, by all appearances, in shambles, Barton has what pop psychology calls a moment of clarity. He finds himself alone on a beach with the waves that have crashed his way throughout the film finally filling the air. Amid the daylight and the waves, he discerns a woman who remarks that "It's a beautiful day." By unreluctantly agreeing, he demonstrates more coherence than he's shown throughout the entire film. He wonders if she's the framed beauty in his room: "Are you in pictures?" She laughs, "Don't be silly." She will not be scrutinized, and she will not be *framed*. This little entertainment is all he knows for now and all he needs to know.

Making a Difference

In *Barton Fink*, we might say, our artist gets ahead of himself. Like most of the Coens' characters he is trying to "make a difference," and it almost inevitably leads to the unleashing of untold horrors. This is the story of such imprisoned souls as William H. Macy's Jerry Lundegaard and Steve Buscemi's Carl Showalter in *Fargo*. They are trying to make good and make right and make sense, and have come to believe (not that they particularly *want* it to be this way) that this is only possible by making large amounts of money. Gabriel Byrne's Tom Reagan (*Miller's Crossing*), Frances McDormand's Marge Gunderson (*Fargo*), and Jeff Bridge's Dude (*The Big Lebowski*) are somehow on the side of the sages, because at their mysterious best, they aren't trying to *make* things happen. You can feel the Coens' respect for them because they know that they don't understand.

In something of a mixture of both character types, we have Billy Bob Thornton's Ed Crane (*The Man Who Wasn't There*), who certainly unleashes the forces of communal destruction by distractedly pursuing the American dream for one twenty-four-hour period, but he seems incapable of even pretending to understand the world around him. He's the barber-mystic (who'd made an appearance or two in the work of Flannery O'Connor), but this time we're allowed into the dry and waterless place that is his mind. Privileged access into the mental agony of Jerry Lundergaard, for instance, is almost too painful to think about, but with Ed Crane, we have a lot of room and almost no inclination to judge. In spite of his folly, Ed Crane possesses the unbearable lightness of paying attention.

As makers, we can say that these captivated souls are *all* artists, but we have to look closely at what their actions create. In trying to articulate the insight of Maurice Blondel on what we might call the politics of making, John Milbank observes that "every action is entirely our own, yet entirely transcends us."[1] That which we call social commentary will modestly try and trace the outworking of such a principle by showing us the states we're in, as well as the states our actions are, despite ourselves, making for ourselves and others. Bluffing ourselves into thinking we're seeing (or making known) the whole will be an occupational hazard. Striving for wholeness (but obviously never *quite* getting there), good social commentary will always be apocalyptic. It will show us our lives and the lives of others hopelessly at the mercy of our *real* values, not the ones we tell ourselves we have. I don't want to reduce their art to less than it is, but is it too much to say that the Coens' storied experiment/illustrations in "making a difference" function as social commentary? And as ever, they can place these lives in front of us, but they can't *make* us look at them. Like Flannery O'Connor, they give us these scandalously wholesome tragicomedies, but it's up to us to apply, to see ourselves, and to wonder how we might, at the very least, not do damage (as we take these tales hilariously *and* seriously) or, better, how to be a healer. At the very least, we might momentarily clear our heads of the Barton Fink feeling.

Love or Money

Fargo is probably one of the most painful portrayals of modern-day American culture we have. It is a chronicle of numerous acts of self-annihilation, but the two we're made to see most vividly are those of Jerry Lundegaard and Carl Showalter. Obliviously presiding over their destruction and his own is Jerry's father-in-law, Wade Gustafson, whose unwillingness to extend his sphere of affection and responsibility to Jerry will unleash the forces of death and destruction. He believes the popular mythology that one's obligations are limited to one's flesh and blood, and he excludes Jerry on a technicality. As Wade sits in front of his daughter's television angrily contemplating his "interests," he presides from a veritable throne of blood.

Although Jerry has already gotten his desperate plan underway, we're given a glimpse of what's brought him this far when Wade, having come around for dinner, sits imponderably in Jerry's home, loathe to express any sentiment beyond displeasure, like a big money-making machine holding the world in contempt. Jerry introduces the topic of one of his own money-making ventures in the hope that Wade might help. As Wade tries to refer him to his accountant, Jerry pulls out his ace-in-the-hole of blood relations: "I'm asking *you* here, Wade. This could work out real good for me and Jean and Scotty—." Wade gives the kiss of death to his family, himself, and numerous bystanders with his hateful response: "Jean and Scotty never have to worry."

This is a complicated situation that Jerry can't even explain to himself. When he hires Carl Showalter and Gaear Grimsrud to kidnap his wife in a desperate money-making venture, they can't understand how or why a man who's married into a wealthy family could ever be compelled to take these measures. What madness demands this mission? Jerry's attempt to articulate his plight shouldn't be too awfully unfamiliar: "Well, it's all just part of this— they don't know I need it, see. Okay, so there's that. And even if they did, I wouldn't get it. So there's that on top, then. See, these're personal matters."

As we watch the destruction ensue, hearing Jerry refer to his scheme with such seemingly moral neutral language as "the deal," "my deal," "this was supposed to be a no rough stuff-type deal," and "a deal's a deal," we can know that we've found ourselves sitting firmly in the realm of apocalyptic. Jerry is one for whom abject fear is a lifestyle, and his barely held-together language of politesse

("Okay . . . Good . . . Real good") is a comedy of terror as it is fever-ishly applied to the machinations of a systemic evil. His desire for security and his well-intentioned drive for gain destroy the lives around him, all methodically traced back to his father-in-law's contempt. We're being carefully shown the moral ambivalence of "the deal" and a powerfully rendered illustration of security as a mortal's chiefest enemy. The Coens bother with these connections. Those who won't will only note that this film contains some violent imagery. Perhaps it's all they're looking for.

How shall we name the motivational spirits the Coens trace before us? Market forces? The power of the air? Are we enslaved to beings that are by nature not gods? Jerry and his wife will be dehumanized to the uttermost. In a tortuously comic scene, we have Jerry, upon walking into the house and seeing that his plan has been carried out, carefully practicing his most convincing tone before phoning his father-in-law, ". . . Wade, it's Jerry, I—we gotta talk, Wade, it's terrible. . . . " Jerry has been so hollowed out in his desire for gain that he no longer knows how to sound emotional. Jean will run handcuffed through the snow with a bag over her head while Jerry explains to Scott, unaware of the irony in his words, that "these men . . . they just want money." We will be shown the chain-reaction of terror spreading through the land and it's modest beginnings in men wanting more money. In time, Jerry will be found trying to flee a hotel in his underwear, squealing like a pig, and Steve Buscemi's Carl will, throughout the film, be put through the machinery like no other character in film history. The Coens are drawing in broad strokes.

A Beautiful Day

All of this is powerfully contrasted with the world-moving presence of Frances McDormand's Marge Gunderson, a child-bearing keeper of law and order who, like no other Coen character, is poetry in motion. Her level-headed look at the horror is upheld by an inexplicable grace and an affection for the little mercies, like her husband Norm's insistence upon making her breakfast the morning of an early morning call. Marge calmly unravels the criminally well-laid plan while stuffing herself on food buffets and Hardees, buying fish bait for her husband, and affirming him in his postal-stamp painting aspirations.

As Jerry, in his impotence, grows more maddeningly aware of himself and the death toll involved in getting ahead, Marge floats, taking it all in without judgment or derision. When they meet, Jerry sits at his desk drawing on a piece of paper the same pattern over and over again, and, in parting, she does allow herself one slight Charlie Meadows-style observation of Jerry's scribbling ineffectiveness, "I'll let you get back to your paperwork there." When they meet again, and Jerry's hopelessly lying demeanor is wearing thin, she gives voice to her buoyantly magnanimous moral authority for one grave moment after he's yelled at her: "Sir, you have no call to get snippy with me. I'm just doin' my job here." In a morally incoherent culture of late capitalism run mad, I suppose we might say that Jerry is doing his job as well, but the genuine civility that Marge embodies in her work has long been more than Jerry can afford. Marge represents a bountifulness (literally and metaphorically) buttressed by gratitude and deep satisfaction with whatever peculiar grace is placed in front of her. And the grace of each day, like the adversity, is sufficient unto itself. Jerry is a mixed-up marionette.

As Marge drives Gaear Grimsrud (the recently murdered Carl Showalter's partner) to the police station, she gives a slow, considered account of all the nightmares faced by the individual victims in the film, and as we should expect from a Coenesque heroine, she does not claim to understand it. If we haven't figured it out already, this is where we will hopefully have the wit to know that we haven't been watching, in the conventional sense, a horror film. Jean and Wade and various bystanders are now dead, and Marge will offer her own calculations concerning the profit margin. She weighs it all out, "And for what? For a little bit of money." This should take us back to Wade Gustafson's dinner visit. Marge weighs in, "There's more to life than money, you know. . . . Don't you know that?" And the truth/beauty/apocalypse that, now and forever, we can take or leave: "And here ya are, and it's a beautiful day. . . ."

For the purposes of apocalyptic, this is probably enough. But the Coens aren't finished with us yet. They've taken us through the proliferating machinery of man's inhumanity to man and revealed, if we're watching, that this is the natural outworking of a purely business world. It is our everyday. But negativity will not even be given the second-to-last word. Maybe we've missed the fact that Marge has been bearing the power of reproduction all through this nightmare vision. She has held the fire of life aloft throughout her journey. The Coens will remind us one more time by showing us Marge and Norm in bed in the most effectively rendered cinematic love scene I know.

In what is probably her most visibly animated moment in the film, Marge passionately explains the importance of Norm's three-cent stamp illustration in the ultimate scheme of things as he finally relents and accepts her proclamation of how proud of him she is: "I love you, Margie."

"I love you, Norm."

They smile at each other. Norm places his hand on Marge's stomach and offers what is, especially in the context of all we've seen, a fearless affirmation of life's joyful persistence, "Two more months." And if the fire of grace still glows within us, we will be moved.

Sometimes There's a Man

Imagining the Zen-like, grace-ridden gaze of deep affection with which Marge Gunderson takes in and responds to the world and following her example is the best way to enjoy *The Big Lebowski*. It is perfectly ridiculous. And perhaps we should place it alongside Robert Bresson's *Au Hasard Balthasar* to best understand what the Coens are up to. Bresson follows the life of a donkey and . . . that's it. Just the donkey. Sometimes there's a donkey. The implication is that a beautiful, worshipful, well-worth-your-time film can be made following a goldfish or a bluejay or a dude. Why? Because all of life is grace, and every detail contains an unfathomable revelation.

This is the perspective of Sam Elliot's character, the Stranger, who is nothing if not impressed. He's never been out to London or France, but this one story is more than enough to satisfy him. The transcendent beauty of it will not be missed on him:

> But I'll tell you what, after seeing Los Angeles and thisahere story I'm about to unfold—wal, I guess I seen somethin' ever' bit as stupefyin' as ya'd see in any a those other places, and in English too, so I can die with a smile on my face without feelin' like the good Lord gypped me.

He is in awe. And he can't explain or even understand it himself except to say, "Sometimes there's a man—I won't say a hee-ro, 'cause what's a hee-ro?—but sometimes there's a man." The Coens are following the one biblical imperative Emily Dickinson claimed to hold to with unwavering obedience: "Consider the lilies."

The Dude has nothing in his appearance, no form or majesty that we should desire him. But we are made to value the Dude highly, which is certainly in keeping with the apocalyptic disposition found so pervasively throughout the Coens' work. A work of exuberant exaltation is, eschatologically speaking, its own credential. Nevertheless, I can't seem to resist a word.

"The bums will always lose!" cries the millionaire, elder Lebowski to his completely unrelated namesake, the Dude. And along with the rich Lebowski (who turns out to be a fake), the forces out to exploit the Dude are the funeral industry, some German nihilists ("Vee belief in nossing, Lebowski! NOSSING!!"), and a maker of pornographic film. All these interactions are sparked at the beginning of the film when a thug, mistaking the Dude for the millionaire Lebowski, breaks into his apartment and urinates on a ratty, old rug which, the Dude insists, "really tied the room together." What follows is a series of haphazard misunderstandings through which the Dude tries, and fails, to put everything in its right place. The Stranger is not unmoved.

As the film ends, the one staple in Lebowski's life is John Goodman's Walter, a Vietnam veteran who inscrutably clings to the Jewish tradition of his ex-wife. ("A tree of life, Dude. To all who cling to it.") Together, they enter into the semifinals of a bowling tournament they've been working toward in between trying to solve a kidnapping fiasco, recover a stolen briefcase, and attend a modern dance recital featuring the Dude's balding, middle-aged landlord, Allan. By way of wrapping things up, the Stranger has this to say: "The Dude abides . . . I don't know about you, but I take comfort in that. It's good knowin' he's out there, the Dude, takin' her easy for all us sinners." I don't know exactly what to make of all this, but as the Dude does not bear scrutiny, I can put my totalizing away and know that I don't have to.

Flannery O'Connor once remarked that she shouldn't receive any credit for turning the other cheek, because her tongue is always in it. Such stratagems are the standard procedure of the Coen brothers in their fabricated prefaces to their published screenplays. Whatever themes we might attribute to their work are anticipated and lampooned in such a way that we're made to feel silly for having presumed much of anything. For *O Brother Where Art Thou?* we have an excerpt from "Carson's Movie Abstract" which is described as "a quarterly of movie synopses compiled for professionals in the humanities." Their ongoing ridicule for the "expert" in all things human ("That Barton Fink feeling") comes at us in their every booby-trapped detail. After a lengthy meditation on modern man as the "box-bound frog" in *O Brother Where Art Thou?* the liberating silliness hits full stride:

> We lie. Death is ours. Art shall discover this lie. But we have changed over the millennia that separate us from the bard whose story we obsessively re-tell. His expeditionaries were small only in relation to giants and the gods; modern man is small, as it were, absolutely. He is frog. His world is dark. And his art, when it is honest, shows him tinged with fear. . . . In its day the whoopee cushion was laughed at; so do we seek to conquer our fear. No doubt the movie film *O Brother Where Art Thou?* will likewise be laughed at, but it is the story, bleak and true, of man in our time.[2]

Like a better-humored Barton Fink (and certainly less simpering), George Clooney's Ulysses Everett McGill has his gift of gab, his confidence, and his passionate search for a treasure that he knows isn't there. There's also his sense of decorum that will not be satisfied without his Dapper Dan Pomade and is completely set on edge at the suggestion of some benevolent, divine presence expecting the thanksgiving *or* repentance of any self-respecting individual. When an old Tiresias-style prophet provides him and his cohorts a ride further down the railroad, he tolerates his pronouncement, but he doesn't have to like it: "And though the road may wind, and yea, your hearts grow weary. Still shall ye foller the way, even unto your salvation."

But Everett does have an appreciation for the paradoxical. This probably has something to do with his own motivations. He's escaped from prison with the help of his two buddies, Delmar and Pete, who assume he's taking them to a buried treasure, or soon-to-be-buried anyway by the impending flooding of the Arktabutta Valley. He maintains that the Tennessee Valley Authority is building a dam that will involve the flooding of the valley (which is true) and that the treasure (which doesn't exist) within the valley will be forever lost. His own hope is to be reunited with his wife, Penny, and his daughters, who've very likely moved on. So there's an indication of some self-understanding in his proclamation that "It's a fool looks for logic in the chambers of the human heart." Whenever he hears tell of or witnesses some inexplicable behavior on the part of his fellow human beings, he'll speculate "Must've been lookin' for answers," and "Everybody's lookin' for answers." But firm commitments are for the weak-minded, and his partners' decision to be baptized is right up there with Tommy Johnson's deal with the devil in terms of tomfoolery. Delmar and Pete were looking to have their sins washed away while Tommy Johnson (a stand-in for Robert Johnson) has given his soul away to the devil in exchange for blues guitar-playing skills like the world has never heard. Everett, in the meantime, prides himself in remaining "unaffiliated."

Like the nihilist Hulga in O'Connor's "Good Country People," he does momentarily fall for the wiles of a Bible salesman ("Folks're lookin' for answers and Big Dan Teague sells the only book that's got 'em"), but John Goodman's Big Dan Teague is a raging fraud who clobbers our travelers and leaves them penniless. Their humiliations have hardly even begun as they push their way through all the paraphernalia of the Depression-era South.

It is characteristic of the Coens to put their people through the redemptive wringer, and in this particular romp, the minister of vengeance is a Sheriff Cooley, who makes enigmatic pronouncements in between chases. As he's having Pete whipped until he gives up the details of Everett and Delmar's final destination, he looks up through his mirrored glasses at the falling rain: "Sweet summer rain. Like God's own mercy."

After a publicized pardon (they've somehow scored a number one radio hit along the way) at a campaign rally coup where the incumbent Pappy O'Daniel soundly outpopularizes his opponent ("Sounds like Homer Stokes is the kinda fella gonna cast the first stone. . . . Well I'm with you folks. I'm a f'give and f'get Christian"), Everett and his boys are sent back on the road by Everett's wife who's insistent that they retrieve her wedding ring. Sheriff Cooley is waiting for them.

Pardon or no pardon, he will have his justice, and the gravediggers sing "You've Got To Walk That Lonesome Valley," as their necks are prepared for hanging and Pete asks God for mercy. With a sense of doom and uncharacteristic loss of speech, Everett quietly protests, "It ain't the law." Cooley intones, "The law. Well the law is a human institution. Perhaps you should take a moment for your prayers."

Everett bows his head. As he prays, the song of the gravediggers increases in volume and intermingles with a low rumbling sound, mournfully groaning and growing gradually in frequency as if it's emerging out from within the earth:

> Oh Lord, please look down and recognize us poor sinners . . . please Lord. . . . I just want to see my daughters again. Oh Lord, I've been separated from my family for so long. . . . I know I've been guilty of pride and sharp dealing. I'm sorry that I turned my back on you, Lord. Please forgive me, and help us, Lord, and I swear I'll mend my way. Let me see my daughters again. Please, Lord, help us. . . . Please help us . . .

The rumbling groan is now an all-consuming roar of water engulfing absolutely everything. Countless tins of Dapper Dan pomade, a noose, a banjo, and various objects of Southern culture. I often view films wondering what Flannery O'Connor, our patron saint of apocalyptic, would make of it all, and I can imagine her remarking that the Coens have just subjected their own movie to a forcible baptizin'.

This is a river-making enterprise, literally and metaphorically, and we find it difficult to deny that death has been swallowed up in the victory of something or other as the pine coffins intended for our boys come bobbing upward to the surface. Pete and Delmar are quick to cry "Miracle!" and "Pity!" It shouldn't surprise us at this point that Everett will have none of it: "It just never fails; once again you two hayseeds are showin' how much you want for intellect. There's a perfectly scientific explanation for what just happened." And in praise of the "perfectly scientific," "No, the fact is, they're flooding this valley so they can hydroelectric up the whole durned state. . . ."

Everett is only getting started in praising the fruits of his skepticism and his hopes for an oddly Matrix-style state:

> Yessir, the South is gonna change. Everything's gonna be put on electricity and run on a payin' basis. Out with the old spiritual mumbo-jumbo, the superstitions and the backward ways. We're gonna see a brave new world where they run everyone a wire and hook us all up to a grid. Yessir, a veritable age of reason—like the one they had in France—and not a moment too soon . . .

All this while floating in God's own mercy and remarking upon the timeliness of the rolltop desk which has just floated up carrying Tommy Johnson and containing what is supposedly the long-sought wedding ring.

In a final affirmation of the futility of fleeing the wisdom unto salvation, he is reunited again with Penny who listens to him praising his own wits while noting that "fate was a-smilin' on me," before informing him that he has the wrong ring. The ring, he realizes, is at the bottom of the newly formed lake, which he's now expected to plumb. While Everett complains of its depths, Penny wryly remarks "The lake wasn't *my* doing . . . ," and Everett's mind is set to working again in a cycle frequently played, seldom remarked.

131

Salt and Light and the Old Spiritual Mumbo-Jumbo

Months before *O Brother Where Art Thou?* was released in America, Nashville was treated to a country music apocalypse at the Ryman Auditorium, former site of the Grand Old Opry, thanks to Joel and Ethan Coen and T-Bone Burnett. Built as a storehouse and broadcasting point for "the old spiritual mumbo-jumbo, the superstitions, and the backward ways," the place has stood mostly vacant for most of my life. In the years since its renovation, many performers have come through and commented on its historical significance, but I highly doubt that its history has ever been so powerfully made manifest as it was the night the Ryman hosted the performers of the *O Brother Where Art Thou?* soundtrack.

In my growing-up years as the Ryman stood empty, I'd been afforded many an apocalyptic moment in the work of T-Bone Burnett, outside the realm of that which most forcibly advertises itself as "Country Music." And I've already had plenty to say about what the Coens have done for me, but the splendor of this evening was almost too much for the mind to hold. As the Country Music Industry embroils itself in blind commercialization, delivering heartless tales with all the moral invigoration of Jerry Springer-style scenarios, two Jewish filmmakers sneak into town and stage a live demonstration of country music's rootedness in the old spiritual mumbo-jumbo, and what is more, the thing was at least a little bit interracial. In fact, it was probably the most redemptive and radically catholic moment the Ryman has ever suffered. My wife and I gaped as one seemingly obscure but historically crucial player was paraded out one after the other. It could hardly have been better if we'd had N. T. Wright and Bono beside us to commentate.

As a sort of homecoming, the cultural significance was nearly deafening. I suspected "Will the Circle Be Unbroken" would make its way into the show, as it did in the end, but what really brought it all back home was Ralph Stanley standing alone at the front of the stage singing "O Death" to a darkened room without musical accompaniment. Something coalesced in that moment, and it was as if Stanley was possessed by a trembling awareness that he was representing more than he could know. Standing and speaking on behalf of an occasionally down-trodden, much-maligned, and enduring "backwoods" culture, his cry announced that death will have no dominion.

Predictably enough, "country radio" ignored the phenomenon as long as it could until sky-rocketing sales became too much of a stumbling block to not try to capitalize upon. But market exploitations aside, the evening and the impulse that made it possible were a sight to behold, a healing river that marketing forces cannot ultimately know or understand. A redemptively American celebration of the utter impossibility of being "unaffiliated." It certainly prepared my mind aptly for the multiethnic, history-bending, all-encompassing answered prayer of Ulysses Everett McGill.

"Jesus, bingo-BINGO!"

Chesterton tells us that the man who steps into the cathedral as a supplicant and the man who enters the brothel as a customer are looking for the same thing. Appreciating the worth of such proposals will require the same humility and wisdom that will view cursing as the lowest form of prayer. The Coens put this insight to use by surrounding their characters' speech with expletives that enhance, rather than deny, the weight of the low, perhaps unintended, prayers. Our words, like our actions, have a power and longevity that exceeds our reckoning. Like O'Connor, the Coens fill their storytelling with images that go beyond their characters' wits and allow their characters words that, like ours, will always transcend their intended meaning. Never a wasted word.

This sense of transcendence in every word and action is uniquely apparent in *The Man Who Wasn't There*. The detached Ed Crane takes in *everything*, but in the estimation of his workaday world, his powers of comprehension are almost nothing. To the consternation of his brother-in-law, with whom he shares the responsibilities of a barbershop, he will dimly take in the announcement that the Russians have exploded an atomic bomb but only show visible frustration at the unseemliness of throwing away human hair: "I mean it's growing, it's part of us. And we cut it off. And throw it away."

133

In Crane's bemused, inarticulate mystification, he bears witness to an order and beauty that his family and friends can sense all the more in his presence. They often detect on the part of Crane a word of rebuke for their unthinking, gluttonous lifestyles, but as ever, Ed sits gazing and listening without words (with the exception of the hair issue) and without comment. In the rare moment when he's about to hazard a word of affection toward his wife, she cuts him off.

In what I believe to be the only appearance of a crucifix in a Coen film, Crane stares peacefully at the image of the crucified Jesus as his wife, Doris, plays bingo in their church sanctuary. In his narration, he notes that Doris probably viewed life everlasting as a nonissue and bingo as the best available option in this one. As he remarks on the tranquility of the place, her number is called and a jubilant cry is heard: "Jesus, bingo-BINGO!"

Robert Bresson tells us that "It is with something clean and precise that you will force the attention of inattentive eyes and ears."[3] *The Man Who Wasn't There* delivers on this principle to the extent that we'll allow it to do its work on us. We're tempted to view Ed Crane with the same inattention he receives from the people around him, puzzled by how unmoved he appears. But the camera tells the better story. Like Crane himself, it points to the great beyond.

Freddy Riedenschneider Sees Daylight

When Crane is lulled out of his sunset-watching, entranced-by-clacking-tree-branches visions long enough to involve himself in a get-rich-quick scheme, it isn't because of discontentment or love of power. He has long been moved by the absent-minded gestures of affection that he occasionally receives from a wife he knows to be unfaithful. As he shaves her legs and regards the shavings floating on the surface of the water, he is seized by an absolute, inarticulate adoration. Tasting a cigarette that's been in her mouth and watching her sleeping form are revelations sufficient unto themselves. Ed Crane is in love.

As ever, the Coens will pay us the tribute of assuming we're able and willing to practice the keen discernment and the negative capability that apocalyptic requires. It's not a trick, after all. But it is admittedly difficult for the film viewer to know how to look properly, or even kindly, when most of what passes before our eyes, media-wise, is designed to titillate in the most aggressive manner possible. In his portrayal of unreflecting love, Billy Bob Thornton has his work cut out for him.

If we'd been made to view moments of tenderness between Jerry and Jean Lundegaard, the nightmare that was made of their lives would have overtaken the rest of *Fargo*. We don't know if Jerry's desire for financial gain might have once been related to a deep-seated affection for his wife. He is impenetrable. But the horrors unleashed by Ed Crane and his hopeful intentions might help us to look back on Jerry more generously. His story might have been told differently, after all. *The Man Who Wasn't There*, like all apocalyptic, is a study in the kind of generous viewing that can tease the mind out of its totalizing tendencies. Of course, the totalizing gaze isn't simply less than generous or immoral; it's scientifically unsound.

We even have a cameo appearance by Heisenberg's Uncertainty Principle, which the Cranes' lawyer, Freddy Riedenschneider, believes might serve to get Doris out of a death sentence:

> You wanna test something, you know, scientifically—how the planets go round the sun, what sunspots are made of, why the water comes out of the tap—well, you gotta look at it. But sometimes, when you look at it, your looking *changes* it. Ya can't know the reality of what happened or what *would*'ve happened if you hadden a stuck in your own godd—n schnozz. So there *is* no "what happened." Not in any sense that we can grasp with our puny minds. Because our minds . . . our minds get in the way. Looking at something changes it . . . Science. Perception. Reality. Doubt . . . Reasonable doubt. I'm sayin', sometimes, the more you look, the less you really know. It's a fact. A proved fact. In a way, it's the only fact there is. This heinie even wrote it out in numbers.

In his opportunistic fashion, Riedenschneider is proposing a possible cure for the Barton Fink feeling. Yet in his near-sighted dedication to his own agenda, establishing reasonable doubt, he joins the rest of the characters in pulling the wool over their own eyes. He is lying out loud, as well as proving Heisenberg's point, when he announces "Freddy Riedenschneider sees daylight."

But only Ed Crane sees daylight, and in a world where he is perceived as the unfeeling sleepwalker, the Coens masterfully reveal that he's the only one who's actually awake. I have to confess that the apocalyptic impact of the film only began to occur to me during the final two or three minutes. But once it overcame my resistance, the world became a different place. Another testament to inarticulate passion, inconsolable longing, and a movingly hapless effort to make the world come out right.

And now we're back in the realms of Ulysses Everett McGill, Tom Reagan, the Dude, Barton Fink and H. I. McDonough. Some are more resistant to the revelation that is everyday than others, but they're up to their necks in it anyway. We sense that Everett knows the score in spite of his denials of the daylight, and his submission to his wife's will might serve as some sort of sanctification in spite of his hard-headedness. Marge Gunderson appears to happily float in the waters most Coen characters spend much of the movie drowning in. And by the end of *The Man Who Wasn't There*, Ed Crane is floating too. When we're made to see as much, we're looking at the Coens' peculiar take on daylight, which is grounded, transcendent, and overflowing with a world made new.

EIGHT

Apocalyptic Xenophilia

An Exercise in Self-Exhortation

Could politics ever be an expression of love?

Ralph Ellison, *Invisible Man*

> Alas! Alas!
> Why, all the souls that were, were forfeit once;
> And He, that might the vantage best have took,
> Found out the remedy. How would you be,
> If He which is the top of judgment, should
> But judge you as you are? O, think on that;
> And mercy then will breathe within your lips,
> Like man new made.
>
> *Measure for Measure* II.ii.72–88

It is not a question of speculation, but of practice. Can these communities of faith (and their ordained leaders) find tongues and ears

137

and will to embrace, articulate, and enact an odd, particular, scandalous mode of reality against the powerful reductionisms all around us? . . . Prophetic speech, that is, the way God's word impinges upon human history, is concrete talk in particular circumstances where the large purposes of God for the human enterprise come down to particulars of hurt and healing, of despair and hope. The synagogue and the church have this demanding, awkward task of claiming much more than can be explained.

Walter Brueggemann, *Texts That Linger, Words That Explode*

As we begin to think through the difference apocalyptic glimpses can and must make in the way we look at the world, as well as what it might mean to live in light of its authority, useful appeal may be made to the work of Shakespeare. In *The Tempest,* the exiled Duke of Milan, Prospero, has the long-sought-for opportunity to exact vengeance upon his enemies. Through his employment of the elemental spirit, Ariel, his stratagems have reduced his foes to a state of sorrow and dismay, and he now holds them in his contemptuous control. But the particulars of their plight and the sadness that grips them do not leave Ariel unmoved. He casually observes as much to Prospero: "Your charm so strongly works 'em/That if you now beheld them, your affections/ Would become tender." An interesting response from a detached principality. Prospero wonders aloud, **"Dost thou think so, spirit?"** Ariel: "Mine would, sir, were I human."

Now it's Prospero's turn to be both moved and redemptively unsettled. If the disembodied spectator is moved to pity, what of the not-without-sin, indisputably incarnate fellow human being? An aloof austerity is hardly an option for one every bit as embroiled in a confused pettiness as his companions. He too has been infected by the power of the air, and, with this in mind, perhaps the throwing of the first stone is a hazardous enterprise. Prospero will redirect his passion toward Ariel's theoretically tender mercies. He will follow his example. His affections will put on flesh:

> Hast thou, which art but air, a touch, a feeling
> Of their afflictions, and shall not myself,
> One of their kind, that relish all as sharply,

138

> Passion as they, be kindlier moved than thou art?
> Though with their high wrongs I am struck to the quick,
> Yet with my nobler reason 'gainst my fury
> Do I take part: The rarer action is
> In virtue than in vengeance.

By choosing "the rarer action," Prospero has stepped down the more excellent path of an enhanced imagination, the purposeful empathy that makes compassion possible. Of course the rarer action is inextricably connected to the rarer disposition of a confessional solidarity in which Prospero notes that he too partakes in the downward spiraling, devastatingly human. He too is an evildoer. His judgments are, he understands, devastatingly finite. In the course of an infinite justice, who should see salvation?

Both the disposition and the action are deeply rooted in the apocalyptic, which appeals to a kingdom, a greater economy than eye-for-eye, tooth-for-tooth and a bigger picture than the narrow vision that will only store up for and strike back on behalf of "me and mine." Apocalyptic testifies concerning a world both beyond *and* presently among the world of appearances, an unveiling of the heretofore ignored meaning with which our words and actions are fraught. In Prospero's disavowal of godlikeness, we sense the triumph of something grander than his sense of what he (or we) most feverishly regard as fair, a prioritizing of grace. Although "struck to the quick," his dignity (and that of his enemies) is elevated above what would have been a tragic failure of the imagination. We can note too that such failures make victims of everyone.

But Shakespeare bears witness to the apocalyptic politics of an imaginative sympathy. When we noted its presence on *The Simpsons*, we summed it up in Miroslav Volf's dictum, "The economy of undeserved grace has primacy over the economy of moral deserts." Taking such principles seriously will require a radical adjustment of vision. For the unimaginative and idolatrous who busy themselves getting and inflicting what is "deserved" while insisting that events mean only what they think they mean, the best thing to hope for is that their faith would be, slowly but surely, undermined. Like nothing else, apocalyptic undermines, driving us to doubt our nervously-defended selves. It mercifully pulls us out of the mental torpor of our already-made-up minds, and when we're looking closely, it is everywhere.

It Lives

In its refusal to anathematize the strange and the unknown, the apocalyptic mind will look hard, humbly, and often happily at what it doesn't understand. Without such looking, one isn't even capable, properly speaking, of seeing or believing much of anything. Without a sense of mystery, we might say, or without the presupposition that the God-given world is, to at least some extent, beyond our grasp, neither worship nor, we might add, a vision of art are possible. Or rather, the objects of worship will always be something less than that which truly sustains life. Anything that teases us out of such idolatrous, closed-minded thinking (whether a falling leaf, the sight of an infant through a window, or a wide-angle shot in a Coen brother film) can be said to be performing the role of apocalyptic.

To put it another way, Madeleine L'Engle was once asked how one might determine whether or not a piece of art, a novel, a play, or whatever is Christian, and her response is worth meditating upon: If it's good, it's Christian. For the believer, there is no "good" unencompassed by what the biblical witness describes as the coming reign of God, and the "secular," eschatologically speaking, doesn't exist. The beautiful, like the truthful, unveils. To expand the concept a little further, we might consider the possibility that all art is apocalyptic. If it's good, it will have the ability to lift us out of one-dimensional thinking, means-end misbehavior, and last ditch power drives that confine our lives. But again, art can't do these things for us. Like poetry, it doesn't *make* anything happen. When it tries to, it probably succumbs to the tight-fisted, control-asserting spirit of propaganda, clearly the opposite of apocalyptic as well as a degenerate form of communication. No amount of hype, production, or record sales can make it otherwise.

Another take on the matter comes to us in an illuminating interview with Woody Allen. While trying to explain the pleasure with which he engages in writing, he notes that he enjoys it for its own sake and that he would surely keep at it even if nobody was willing to fund his work. It's an exercise in creative edification, and he explains why he tries not to worry too much about the attention it will or won't receive: "Because if there's anything of value there, it will live; and if there's not, better it shouldn't. That's one of the nice things about writing, or any art; if the thing's real, it just lives."[1]

We might add that, if it doesn't, what's the point? If it doesn't challenge or undermine our deathly egocentrism, why bother? And if we aren't looking to be rescued from such straitjackets, what are we doing? The apocalyptic gesture, like the human face properly gazed upon, can unlock unforeseen possibilities. Franz Kafka suggests that if reading a literary text doesn't facilitate a skull-hammering awakening, we're wasting our time. To accept the full revelation of artistic expression is to endure an ice-axe that, in Kafka's imagery, can crack the frozen seas inside us all. This is the language that comes to mind when I think of apocalyptic living, the unexpected, new-every-morning lifestyle of bearing witness of another dimension beyond "just deserts," maximum exploitation, and whatever reductionisms keep our minds enthralled.

Apocalyptic Baby

When we refuse to look apocalyptically, our lives become bored, depressed, and mean. We also find it difficult to think or imagine beyond ourselves or whatever we term the "interests" of our own family, friends, and culture. Going to the trouble of wondering what it might be like to exist outside of the class or country within which we happen to have been born becomes a task we wouldn't dream of undertaking even as we resent the suggestion that we should. This is what my colleague, Thomas Hayes, calls a "selective fundamentalism." We choose our die-hard stands to suit our lifestyles and our prejudices. Our absolute truths and values, our nonnegotiables, conveniently coincide with whatever lives we're already living and whatever decisions we've already made. The apocalyptic mind will resist surrendering to this tendency while noting that it's an imprisonment to which we are born. Being disabused of this surrounding insanity is a big part of what "being saved" will mean.

As the examples we've examined demonstrate, the heartfelt laughter of self-directed humor (like all sympathetic portrayals of human failure) isn't a bad place to start. Without empathy, there is no understanding. In an address to a group of artists at the Thalia Theatre in Hamburg, Germany, Bono offers a meditation on the painful seriousness of fascism and the apocalyptic antidotes made available in the artistic counterenvironments of an "emphatic imagination":

> Laughter is the evidence of freedom. . . . It was from a Mel Brooks movie called *The Producers* that U2 took the name of their last album. In the bizarre musical an S.S. officer is met with the greeting "Achtung, baby!" to which he replies, "Ze furher would never say *baby*!" Quite right. The furher would never say *baby*. We are writers, artists, actors, scientists. I wish we were comedians. We would probably have more effect. "Mock the devil and he will flee from thee." "Fear of the devil leads to devil worship." Anyway, for all this: imagination. To tell our stories, to play them out, to paint pictures, moving and still, but above all *to glimpse another way of being*. Because as much as we need to describe the world we do live in, we need to *dream up the kind of world we want to live in*. In the case of a rock & roll band that is to dream out loud, at high volume, to turn it up to eleven. Because we have fallen asleep in the comfort of our freedom.[2]

The anal retentiveness that can't say *baby*, entrenched in the bipolar thinking of "us vs. them," is threatened by the life-giving spirit of an imagination that speaks truth to power. It will find apocalyptic offensive and deeply problematic because its own world is absolutely sure and unproblematic. The tightness is an absence of elasticity and good humor strengthened by its conviction that it already knows almost everything worth knowing, the despair that calls itself "realism." Apocalyptic makes us more repentantly aware of reality and relieves us of the need to demonize, or ignore altogether, the odd and the unknown.

The apocalyptic believer goes out of her way to have such pristine hardness overcome because she knows that it cannot ultimately sustain life. She is haunted by what she might miss if she doesn't talk to homeless people or ever try to make a home of any culture other than her own. She is wary of her immediate world's frequent inability (or unwillingness) to extend respect or accord value beyond itself. She understands her moral obligation to think and imagine further. Sanity requires as much.

An increased elasticity, interpersonally and internationally, will require an apocalyptic humility of mind that eschews its own egocentrism as well as its defensive sense of what's rational. An informed humility knows that reason can only grasp so much, and it will not reject as out of hand or irrelevant everything outside of reason's grasp. To do so is to be impenetrably resistant to the logic-defying God as well as the not-to-be-compartmentalized people and cultures that populate our environment.

Something of the imaginative sympathy required in this sense-restoring surrender is effectively captured in William Stringfellow's meditation on listening:

> Listening is a rare happening among human beings. You cannot listen to the word another is speaking if you are preoccupied with your appearance or impressing the other, or if you are trying to decide what you are going to say when the other stops talking, or if you are debating about whether the word being spoken is true or relevant or agreeable. Such matters may have their place, but only after listening to the word as the word is being uttered. Listening, in other words, is a primitive act of love, in which a person gives self to another's word, making self accessible and vulnerable to that word.[3]

We are, in fact, made for this kind of listening *and* this kind of viewing. When we're committed to a necessarily nondefensive, apocalyptic receptivity we will see new life bursting through in everything from a pig founding a community of outcasts by rescuing a dog who is trying to kill him in *Babe: Pig in the City* to a lone couple ushering in a new day by overcoming fearful normalcy with new dance steps in *Strictly Ballroom*. Life won't be confined to our expectations, so we better get used to it. And if we get what's coming to us, in the cosmic sense, we will be made to listen and look this way whether we like it or not. Hopefully, it won't involve the drastic means through which O'Connor and the Coens get their characters to the point of epiphany, but we can be rather hard. In my own life, a well-placed child can often do the trick when I'm half awake, but within minutes, I'm back in the machine, desperately in need of another reminding. If O'Connor is to be believed, some jolt designed to get us listening and looking again is strategically placed around every corner in the ongoing apocalyptic that is everyday. Is anyone paying attention?

The Political Significance of the Unexpected Response

"The discoverer of the role of forgiveness in the realm of human affairs was Jesus of Nazareth."[4] These words from Hannah Arendt offer a useful scholarly assessment that can help us to understand Jesus as the initiator of a new way of being in the world. His historical significance as a Palestinian peasant whose movement, like a chain-reaction, overcomes the Roman-occupied world strikes us with new force when we note that, ethnically and politically, he was born into a kind of slave status (choose your racial slur). And when we then think of apocalyptic as an invitation to reimagine reality, the exalted language of Revelation, which describes Jesus as the Alpha and the Omega, is freed to do its work of announcing that the cosmos isn't quite what we think it is. Glory, honor, power, and praise are radically different from what we have in mind. The peasant is making all things new.

I hasten to add, for the sake of clarity, that Jesus was faithfully radicalizing the Jewish imagination. The impulse of apocalyptic goodwill is made manifest throughout Old Testament history and literature in, for example, Joseph's kind reception of his brothers, Jeremiah's admonition to Israel to seek the welfare of their captors' culture, Jonah's bitter wrestling with what he takes to be God's overly indulgent valuing of a corrupt Nineveh, and Isaiah's imagery suffering servant as well as his eschatological hopes, peppered throughout the Hebrew prophets, of a coming day when:

144

> The wolf shall live with the lamb,
> the leopard shall lie down with the kid,
> the calf and the lion and the fatling together,
> and a little child shall lead them . . .
> They will not hurt or destroy on all my holy mountain;
> For the earth will be full of the knowledge of the Lord
> As the waters cover the sea (11:6–9).

Jesus inherited and, we might say, popularized the alternative social ethic of a new world on the way, sometimes latent (and thereby receiving the counterwitness of the prophets) and sometimes powerfully manifest in Jewish history. For the pagan world especially, Jesus was the prototype of a new social datum, and its infectious presence can be discerned in everything we term "apocalyptic." As his teachings, his political career, and his execution make clear, he was no detached theorist sending his followers to an ineffective, idealistic, dandelion-hugging doom. His vocation was one of full-bodied apocalyptic.

If "God" then is to be more than the word we use as shorthand to describe what we prefer to believe, there will be tension between what we're doing and settling for and the in-break of divine revelation, the good purposes of God. Otherwise we aren't looking to be *saved* from anything more than, say, guilt feelings or a fear of "the afterlife." Living within the tension and learning to look for it in media, relationships, and the language we use will call for sobriety and a skepticism borne by humility. Without apocalyptic, the tension escapes our notice, and we're left to satisfy ourselves, neurotically, with the unchallenged, this-is-the-way-it-has-to-be status quo.

The unexpected response of a holy deity to a rebellious creation is the longsuffering, culture-transforming Jesus whose newness challenges the norms of human relationships. The unexpected responses that subjects of the coming kingdom are invited to embody (and thereby represent a new age within the present one) are perhaps best encompassed by Oliver O'Donovan's term "xenophilia." Broadband apocalyptic will work its way into every aspect of existence with the biblical imperative of a more imaginative magnanimity: "Xenophilia is commanded us: the neighbor

145

whom we are to love is the foreigner whom we encounter on the road."[5]

Such magnanimity (the rarer action) has a way of changing things. Historically speaking, Christianity has a rather bad reputation for cold-hearted fault-finding in its assessment of media, culture, and trends. It's as if such religious faith has no greater calling than counting the bad words, spotting the sexual innuendo, and walking away in a loud, well-publicized huff. In contrast, apocalyptic xenophilia responds redemptively, which isn't to say that it *brings* redemption or that it does the redeeming. Instead, it *sees* and *affirms* the redemption already present and already underway. It is *looking* for it. Xenophilia is the way of affirmation.

The prototypical lifestyle of an apocalyptically-based intelligence will include such markings as what Marva Dawn calls "hilarity" and what Yoder calls "revolutionary subordination." It can unexpectedly affirm more than most because it appeals to a more spacious reality (what is and was and is to come) than whatever fevered passions possess an instant, a culture, or an era. It will out-affirm, out-believe, and out-value whatever it beholds. It will find bridges *out of* Babylon in every quarter. The apocalyptic response will often take the form of an improvised reimagining of the given, and its practitioners in recent history include Dorothy Day, Oscar Romero, Martin Luther King Jr., Vaclav Havel, Lech Walesa, the Berrigan brothers, and the lone student facing down a row of tanks in Tiananmen Square.

The words and actions associated with these figures have a way of expanding the sphere of what's considered historically possible. They testify to a transcendence in everyday activity with an earth-bound agility that interpenetrates all that appears mundane and insignificant. In this state of affairs, every exchange is full of poetic possibility, and as John Milbank puts it, "Every action begins to be a consequence. In aiming for a goal, it also emanates."[6] If we take the resurrection of Jesus as an operative principle, we can be assured that God will not let the apocalyptically faithful word, action, or life amount to nothing. It will have cosmic meaning. This is the comfort and promise and renewed moral invigoration of John's Revelation to the early Christians.

This is the political significance of the unexpected response, the creative confrontation of divine generosity applied to culture and concrete scenarios. As Oliver O'Donovan defines this engagement, "Generosity means: not staying within the limits which public rationality sets on its approval of benevolence. An extravagant, unmeasured goodness, corresponding to God's own providential care, defies the logic of public expectation."[7] Extravagant kindness of action (as well as interpretation) amounts to apocalyptic disruption of whatever norms currently crown themselves as "realistic," "prudent," or "appropriate." These confrontations bring onto the scene an indiscriminate generosity that will often appear supernatural and scandalous as they necessarily go beyond what has appeared previously available or reasonable.

Then as now, we can note that the human response to such divine revelations will often be "Crucify him." Jesus' summons holds no guarantee of short-term effectiveness or immediate gratification. But as Arendt maintains, Jesus' career constituted an inbreak in human history, and the long-term victory of this inbreak is implemented whenever power constellations are creatively and redemptively engaged. Whether in Selma, Belfast, Prague, or Tiananmen Square, the witness outweighs the opposition's present imaginings. The engagement is an open-handed invitation to a better ethic than whatever the oppressor, committed to a blueprint of self-destruction, has deemed "necessary."

As we move further toward the concept of apocalyptic living, we can add, using John Milbank's phrase, that it is "grounded in a refusal of the contrast between my interest and that of the other."[8] By imagining beyond such *shalom*-denying contrasts, the apocalyptic sees more and further down the road. The radical witness of this very different economy has a way of relativizing our perceived have-to's, our interests, and (perhaps most liberating of all for our own culture) our rights.

Prepare To Be Authentic

Apocalyptic action is made possible by a hopeful watchfulness. This disposition is inherently distrustful of any either/or, have-to, or trigger-happy response, and it is deeply aware of our tendency to unimaginatively assume that we're trapped in a script of only one of two options. The apocalyptic disposition, committed to the enemy-loving generosity that presents itself as God's historical self-disclosure, is sustained through a prayerfully imaginative receptivity toward options unrecognized by the reigning and ordinary machinery of social interaction. The action, whether improvised or well-practiced, will body forth new possibilities and, in apocalyptic terms, participate in the ushering in of a new world.

If loving one's enemy is a political act (and I don't see how it could be anything but), maybe we can call it an artistic decision as well. It will be the daily, mostly unromantic application of a new creation, a new habit of being in the rigidly mechanical realm of human relations, and it will often be costly. But according to the biblical tradition, it is a new birth to a life of hope of which Jesus is the pioneer, and its way of constituting a historical newness, whatever its context, is what gives meaning to words like "witness," and "testimony." The bigger authenticity of a better reality is made known.

Bearing witness, testifying, and remaining watchful will involve leaving no medium unengaged. For Flannery O'Connor, there is no personality, billboard, sunset, or peacock unworthy of engagement. Beck acknowledges that he finds television too overwhelming to entertain because he wouldn't be able to turn it off. He finds it all too interesting. Apocalyptic is unendingly interested. It believes, hopes, and endures. And it looks everywhere.

In the case of media, engagement is a necessity. If we don't talk about what we're watching and hearing and taking in, we're really only addicts, taking in information without response. When we surrender our attention without thinking critically (not necessarily negatively), the victory of a death-dealing matrix over our lives is nearly complete. Unless we talk back and talk about what passes before us, we're pretty well finished, and the daily becomes a repulsive burden. Authenticity implies engagement. And as ever, it's easy to get started once two or more are gathered. It could be that no film, music, literature, or television is so patently bad that it can yield no worthwhile conversation. Assuming that there's no point in discussing something is probably good news for the Matrix.

On the subject of matrix-denying breakthroughs, I'd like to offer a chronicle or two. I've made mention of various figures in recent history who've embodied, in some fashion, apocalyptic lifestyle decisions, and I will now mention some everyday particulars. It will be obvious that these stories take place outside the atmosphere of life-or-death scenarios, but they are openings into an apocalyptically-founded morality, a summons to be more awake and alive. Although modest, we have to start somewhere. The new humanity has nowhere else to happen but here, and authenticity springs eternal every once in awhile.

Suburban Apocalyptic

One of my earliest memories features my brother and me being pelted repeatedly by gravel rocks. I can't recall if we'd done or said anything to provoke the attack, but I vividly recall that the neighbor child was much older than we were and the aggression was like nothing we'd seen or known before. We were confounded and afraid.

We ran. But before gathering much speed, I picked up one of the rocks that lay scattered at our feet and threw it helplessly in the direction of our attacker. When we made it into our house, amid our tearful complaints and wild-eyed retelling, my mother had one question: Did you throw any rocks? Already well-versed in the politics of eye-for-an-eye, I begrudgingly admitted that one rock had been thrown, but I couldn't see how that had anything to do with the terror to which we'd just been subjected.

As my mother accompanied me to the home of the neighbor child, she didn't explain that we were holding to the ancient, long-practiced wisdom of what John Howard Yoder calls "evangelical nonconformity," and she didn't note that, as people of the apocalypse, we will follow the slain lamb wherever he goes in a world we mustn't try to control. But I knew that I should have known what that one rock would get me, because I'd long understood that, as my mother might have put it, "We do things differently." I was made to apologize to my neighbor for the one rock, and she didn't have to tell me that no description of the veritable rock shower that preceded it would be allowed.

I wouldn't seek baptism for many years to come, but when I did, I knew that I was publicly submitting to the apocalyptic social ethic to which this kind of conflict resolution points. It was a meta-narrative in which I'd been immersed since before I knew what to call it. In my neighborhood and at school, my experiences would take on a different flavor after I'd discussed them with my family. No so-called friendship that required the denying of another friendship could be worthy of the name, and any joy that required the exclusion of a peer would be forever illegitimate. There is an exuberant communion whose ecstasies exceed the triumph of the high school clique. I was made to understand that God's movement would happen (was happening) with or without me, but I also knew that I probably shouldn't consider myself an affiliate without having consented to it. All through my childhood the question of my consent was never a matter of "if," but "when." The pattern of apocalyptic-style living was ever before me.

Give It Away

I have a painter friend whom I will refer to as Jasper. His work is met with tremendous enthusiasm by any and all who come around to his showings or see his work displayed around town, but he is notoriously unwilling to position himself in the manner that, it is believed, would advance his career. One of my friends once asked me if I thought Jasper might accept his services as a manager, and I knew he probably wouldn't, but I had trouble finding the words to explain why not.

Apart from his reluctance to worry my friend with his affairs (and to worry himself with my friend's worrying), Jasper counts among the temptations to be resisted the drive to try and make things happen. His understanding of his artistic vocation is inextricably bound to his commitment to the radically countercultural mind-set of trying to be, in view of God's care, anxious for nothing and not holding on too tightly to anything at all. Jasper believes that the only way we can gain our lives is by losing them, and managerial assistance, I assumed, would strike him as trying a little too hard to grasp and gain. In view of God's sparrow-feeding, hair-counting generos-

150

ity, he believes that there is no such thing as a missed opportunity; God will sort it all out. My friend's response was a telling study in contrasts: "That's funny. I view *everything* as a missed opportunity."

Over time, Jasper has been only too happy to receive the help of folks who take it to be their privilege to place their gifts alongside his and assist his work in whatever way they can. In fact, he'd be the first to tell you that his life would be impossible without such help. But the trouble comes when the proffered assistance is a little less good-naturedly disinterested than it first appears. Enter Jasper's occasion for an apocalyptic response.

We'll call Jasper's art dealer friend Frank. Having facilitated some showings for Jasper (out of which he took an ample percentage), Frank was alarmed to note that Jasper often chose to show and sell his art outside of Frank's purview. With no legal recourse with which to capitalize upon Jasper's successes apart from his involvement, Frank would describe these independent efforts as acts of betrayal and ingratitude and would often maintain (to Jasper and anyone else who'd listen) that he owes his career to him. Responding redemptively to this relationship (or any relation) is an artistic endeavor in itself.

When Frank appeared at Jasper's studio with a wealthy art buyer, Jasper understandably felt trapped. If the buyer takes an interest, Frank's you-owe-me case against Jasper is strengthened, and whatever happens, it seems that Jasper's relationship with the art buyer is, from the outset, compromised. Sure enough, the buyer comments upon a particular piece with pleasure.

"Do you like it? Here. I want you to have it. I insist." Now something beautiful has occurred. The buyer is moved by the gesture in such a way that a relationship is begun; the kind of relationship, by the way, that keeps Jasper believing his art isn't, in fact, a waste of time. And Frank is confronted with a choice that, if my guess is correct, feels an awful lot like the end of a Flannery O'Connor story. He can either view his effort as a failed stratagem ("Curses! Foiled again") or a mission accomplished in which he's connected a friend with another friend and watched them become friends. Like most apocalyptic gestures, Jasper's move can be viewed either as an opening to a better world or the heaping of burning coals.

151

Apocalyptic Acumen

Both of these incidents are walked along the tightrope of apocalyptic acumen. The actors base themselves in what the biblical tradition recognizes as God's apocalyptic presence in human affairs. As O'Connor's Misfit understands, this disclosure changes the playing field of social relations for all time, and its implementation will involve actions in which grace *really* reigns, not simply the forgiveness of sins for me and mine. N. T. Wright has compared this insane reduction of the gospel to a deranged postal carrier whose career is marked by the presumption that all the packages and letters with which he's been entrusted are his own. When we suffer under such mad misunderstandings of what we've been called to embody, we won't really look at or live within the world any differently than anyone else, except perhaps to bear a certain unimaginative smugness in much that we think and do.

To look and act apocalyptically is to do more than merely offer a verbal affirmation of a coming day. The witness says Yes as well as No. Yes to the redemptive purposes to which America is called (and which it sometimes answers) but No to the suggestion that it is deserving of worship or uncritical devotion. Yes to the kindness that Frank is capable of embodying in Jasper's life but No to the power-mongering manipulations that try to impose a sense of debt and guilty obligation. To attempt to be the agent of incarnate witness is to live in humble acknowledgment of the new creation already underway without knowing entirely (or how to best articulate) its full implications. The stumblings and false starts that come with these shots at authenticity are part of a troubled, earthenware-vesseled legacy and lifestyle. A close look at early church history will show that such struggles are the stuff of a prototypically Christian existence.

As the work of John Howard Yoder has shown, the committed, other-centered discernment of the New Testament's believing community demonstrates a prioritizing of new creative unity that served as a sign of an unheard of, peculiar peoplehood in the first-century world. Their whole-body efforts to live in a manner worthy of the new authenticity (pioneered by Jesus and empowered by his resurrection) are marked by their determination to take the

152

newness into everyday realities. When we note their willingness to forego dietary habits, social hierarchies, and material possessions in an effort to maintain their unity as a new kind of family, we might wonder what unused methods of witness we've failed to recognize as the proper tasks of apocalyptic. We'll recall Chesterton's adage that Christianity hasn't been tried and found wanting; it's been found difficult and therefore left untried.

An apocalyptic worldview is hardly possible without the exercise of a communal imagination from which inspiration is drawn. Sharing these stories and recalling moments of success *and* failure in the practice of an embodied faith while repenting of the times we neglected the better way for what seemed like the easier way is one of the works (and joys) of the gathered community. The training takes place within and for the sake of friendships. This *ekklesia* remains perpetually open to entry and admonition from outside itself because it knows, by it's own self-definition, that it doesn't own the copyright on God, his kingdom, or the new humanity it seeks to represent. Oliver O'Donovan explains this radical call to other-centeredness well:

> It can exist only as a community that is always gathering, anticipating the final state in which mankind as a totality will gladly be subject to the rule of God. This is what should be meant when, in the context of the formal dogmatic definition, the church is described as "catholic": the church leaps over all existing communal boundaries and forbids any part of the human race—even the church itself, as presently gathered and structured—to think of the Kingdom of God as confined within its own limits and to lose interest in what lies beyond them.[9]

No Eye Has Seen

For all of its apparent exuberance, borderline exaggeration, and ecstatic anticipation of a new world interpenetrating and informing this one, the apocalyptic mind also knows that it doesn't know much, or, to borrow O'Connor's language, it understands that it doesn't understand. As Paul attests, perhaps alluding to Isaiah, it knows that no eye has seen, nor ear heard, nor human heart conceived the details of God's future. It also knows, with Paul, that the failure to acknowledge our own ignorance (and to take up a necessary, healthy agnosticism on certain matters) can get us in the habit of demonizing that which we fear or find hard to understand. At the very least, the apocalyptic mind knows (with Muggeridge and *The Simpsons*) that our best intentions and our finest accomplishments are shabby and laughable compared to what we somehow know we're made for, and defensively crowning them as the absolute best will blind us to and protect us from the truly awesome, which is to say, the truly apocalyptic.

To be sure, whatever ethic or lifestyle we're tempted to settle for might appear unprecedentedly good, in the historical sense, and it may be, as much of Western civilization is, unmistakably dependent upon the Jewish and Christian transmission. But the apocalyptic witness, within the transmission, is what keeps us redemptively unsettled and forever straining forward to what lies ahead while holding fast to the indestructible life already lived and already conquering in the risen Jesus. Apocalyptic is moving, and the carefully considered speech adequate to the movement will often be a mobile army of metaphors that testify to more than it can ever hope to master. The biggest words of awe, goodness, and cosmic meaning will be reserved for the glimpses, all around us, of the already/not yet apocalypse. It will see the "vast construction" of O'Connor's *Wise Blood* vision in the starry starry sky and a supernatural significance in every human face and every grain of sand.

This is the sensibility that comes to mind when I hear Laurie Anderson speak of her father's death as an entire library burning down or Francois Mauriac's declaration that every drop of human blood is of infinite value. The practitioner of an apocalyptic worldview understands that she doesn't know what she's dealing with entirely when she regards another person, nor does she know, fully, what she's looking at when she gazes into a mirror. The moral implications of such a mind-set are, as the historical impact of the biblical story has shown, revolutionary. The human being, as a bearer of the divine image, becomes too mysterious to mishandle. When humans start looking at each other this way (especially in an age of slavery, target markets, statistics, unpersons, and collateral damage), nothing is ever the same again. When you're looked upon as a living mystery or a living library or a bearer of incalculable value, you're in the presence of an apocalyptic gaze and the exaltation of "the least of these," which may be the only fully functional humanism the world has ever known.

Superaliveness

In describing her pilgrimage to Rome, Flannery O'Connor did not leave behind her peculiar, utterly-unimpressed-with-superficiality opinion on matters, but she did apply the word "holiness," which she defines as "special superaliveness."[10] Given our tendency to compartmentalize and separate whatever we mean by "spiritual" from everyday experience, this is a much-needed corrective to an all-too-prevalent Gnostic theology. The existence of a category like "spiritual issues" speaks powerfully to the failure of the self-proclaimed inheritors of the biblical tradition to connect the story, made boring through some unholy miracle, to actual human bodies, perhaps especially their own. The word tragically protected from flesh, to paraphrase Wendell Berry, fails to arrive at a proper ordering of the affections and renders all infertile.

As I've maintained throughout the present work, apocalyptic breaks through the "spiritual," the "personal," the "private," the "religious," and whatever mad categories have kept a necessarily incarnate faith in an incorporeal state. It serves as a remedy by freeing the captive imagination from its sentimentalizing, "deep down in your heart" reductionisms. It extends and demands a deeply imaginative charity that transcends and scandalizes all our tired understandings of "good." The summons is to a scandalous superaliveness that thinks and acts differently.

The possibility of actually acting differently can be kept at some conveniently impossible distance from our everyday consideration as long as we keep Jesus "spiritual." We can view him as a kind of phantom friend who absolves us of our guilt feelings, expands our territory, and promises to take our "souls" to a faraway place when we die, just so long as we ask him into our "hearts" as the savior of our "spiritual" selves. There's a lot of money to be made in this sort of nonsense, and it certainly has a way of filling up meeting spaces on Sunday mornings. But it doesn't bear any resemblance to any recognizable orthodoxy within the historical Christian faith. It is, rather, the almost purposefully useless, deliberately short-sighted, politically irrelevant religion that will often inspire contempt among honest people.

The apocalyptic believer will be light-heartedly aware of the inadequacy of even her most heartfelt words and expressions, as well as her natural tendency to shrink-wrap the revelation into more easily digestible and manageable forms. This is the healthy skepticism and suspicion that begins with self-doubt and extends itself to doubting the be-all-end-all claims of one's own culture. A fully "spiritualized" Jesus will never challenge these claims, but the Jesus of John's Revelation does and thereby relativizes, without denying, all the lesser beauties that elicit our distracted claims of "awesome." When we read Revelation attentively, we will feel all our presumptions, idolatries, and shrink-wrap giving way to a newness we cannot control or fully understand.

In my own debilitating tendency to read the Bible as if it says what I already know and believe instead of reading it repentantly with a mind ready to yield to transformation, I need whatever I can get my hands on to better get my head around the meaning of indefatigable, irrefutable, and embarrassingly credible apocalyptic. If it doesn't challenge my preconceived notions in any way, if its superaliveness doesn't leave me chastened, I'm probably not looking at it properly. Our inclination to run from the shocking grace that will transform our lives and our world is difficult to overestimate, but the superaliveness, like apocalyptic, is irrepressible. All shall be made alive with laughter. It unveils, before our eyes, the not-to-be-mastered whole of a world without end.

Notes

Chapter 1

1. Quoted in David Toole, *Waiting for Godot in Sarajevo: Theological Reflections on Nihilism, Tragedy, and Apocalypse* (Boulder: Westview Press, 1998), 92.

2. Flannery O'Connor, *The Habit of Being*, ed. Sally Fitzgerald (New York: Noonday Press, 1979), 79.

3. N. T. Wright, *Jesus and the Victory of God* (Minneapolis: Fortress Press, 1996), 176.

4. John Milbank, *Theology and Social Theory: Beyond Secular Reason* (Malden, Mass.: Blackwell, 1993), 171.

5. J. R. R. Tolkien, *The Lord of the Rings* (Boston: Houghton Mifflin Company, 1987), 5.

6. Andrey Tarkovsky, *Sculpting in Time: Reflections on the Cinema*, trans. Kitty Hunter-Blair (Austin: University of Texas Press, 1986), 42.

7. Quoted in G. B. Caird, *The Revelation of St. John the Divine* (London: Adam & Charles Black, 1966), 2.

8. Ibid., 27.

9. Ibid., 19.

10. Ibid., 76.

11. Ibid., 83.

12. Ibid., 129.

13. Ibid., 137.

14. William T. Cavanaugh, *Torture and Eucharist* (Malden, Mass.: Blackwell, 1998), 5.

15. Caird, *St. John the Divine*, 263.

Chapter 2

1. Flannery O'Connor, *The Complete Stories* (New York: Farrar, Straus, and Giroux, 1971), 132.

2. O'Connor, *The Habit of Being*, 221.

3. Harold Bloom, *How to Read and Why* (New York: Scribner, 2000), 52.

4. O'Connor, *The Habit of Being*, xiii

5. Ibid., 118.

6. Ibid., 116.

7. Ibid., 145.

8. Flannery O'Connor, *Wise Blood* (New York: Farrar, Straus, and Cudahy, 1962), 16.

9. O'Connor, *The Habit of Being,* 172

10. Ibid., 70.

11. O'Connor, *The Complete Stories,* 113.

12. Ibid., 115

13. O'Connor, *The Habit of Being,* 178.

14. Ibid., 187.

15. Ibid., 180.

16. Ibid., 147.

17. Flannery O'Connor, *Mystery and Manners,* ed. Sally and Robert Fitzgerald (New York: Noonday Press, 1970), 10–13.

18. J. P. de Caussade, *Self-Abandonment to Divine Providence,* trans. Algar Thorold (London: Burns, Oates, and Washbourne, 1933), 81.

19. O'Connor, *The Habit of Being,* 137.

20. O'Connor, *The Complete Stories,* 245.

21. Ibid., 165.

22. Ibid., 168.

23. Ibid., 174.

24. Ibid., 46.

25. Ibid., 47.

26. O'Connor, *The Habit of Being,* 59.

27. Flannery O'Connor, *The Violent Bear It Away* (New York: Farrar, Straus, and Cudahy, 1960), 221.

28. Ibid., 230.

29. Ibid., 241–42.

30. O'Connor, *The Habit of Being,* 163–4.

31. Ibid., 126.

32. Ibid., 214.

33. Ibid., 227.

34. Ibid., 163.

35. Ibid., 57.

Chapter 3

1. Jean Bethke Elshtain, *Real Politics: At the Center of Everyday Life* (Baltimore: Johns Hopkins University Press, 1997), 9.

2. *William F. Buckley & Malcolm Muggeridge on Faith and Religious Institutions* (New York: The National Committee of Catholic Laymen, 1981), 40–43.

3. Jonathan Swift, "The Battle of the Books," in *The Writings of Jonathan Swift,* ed. Robert A. Greenberg and William Bowman Piper (New York: Norton and Co., 1973), 375.

4. Mikhail Bakhtin, *Rabelais and His World,* ed. and trans. Helene Iswolsky (Bloomington: Indiana University Press, 1984), 11–12.

5. Walker Percy, *Signposts in a Strange Land,* ed. Patrick Samway (New York: Farrar, Straus, and Giroux, 1991), 415.

6. Quoted in Elshtain, *Real Politics,* 5.

7. Wendell Berry, *What Are People For?* (San Francisco: North Point Press, 1990), 90.

8. Eugene Peterson, *Reversed Thunder* (San Francisco: Harper and Row, 1988), 171.

9. Berry, *What Are People For?* 139.

10. Miroslav Volf, *Exclusion and Embrace: A Theological Exploration of Identity, Otherness, and Reconciliation* (Nashville: Abingdon Press, 1996), 85.

11. G. K. Chesterton, *Chaucer* (New York: Farrar & Rinehart, 1932), 213.

Chapter 4

1. Catherine Pickstock, *After Writing: On the Liturgical Consummation of Philosophy* (Malden, Mass.: Blackwell, 1998), 4.

2. William Stringfellow, "How My Mind Has Changed," in *A Keeper of the Word: Selected Writings of William Stringfellow,* ed. Bill Wylie Kellermann (Grand Rapids: Eerdmans, 1994), 81.

3. John Howard Yoder, "Why Ecclesiology Is Social Ethics," in *The Royal Priesthood: Essays Ecclesiological and Ecumenical,* ed. Michael G. Cartwright (Grand Rapids: Eerdmans, 1994), 123.

4. Nick Kent, "Happy Now?" *Mojo,* June 2001 <http://www.followmearound.com/press/124.html>.

5. Oliver O'Donovan, *The Desire of the Nations: Rediscovering the Roots of Political Theology* (New York: Cambridge University Press, 1996), 76.

6. "Thom Yorke—The Full Interview" <http://www.nme.com/features/29006.htm>

Chapter 5

1. Claude Tresmontant, *Christian Metaphysics,* trans. Gerard Slevin (New York: Sheed and Ward, 1965), 99–101.

Chapter 6

1. Marshall McLuhan with Wilfred Watson, *From Cliche to Archetype* (New York: Viking Press, 1970), 149.

2. Walter Wink, *Naming the Powers: The Language of Power in the New Testament* (Philadelphia: Fortress, 1984), 84

3. Mark Kemp, "Where It's At Now," *Rolling Stone,* 17 April 1997.

4. Quoted in Hans Urs von Balthazar, *Bernanos: An Ecclesial Existence,* trans. Erasmo Leiva-Merikakis (San Francisco: Ignatius Press, 1996), 204.

5. Quoted in Paul Virilio, *The Art of the Motor,* trans. Julie Rose (Minneapolis: University of Minnesota Press, 1995), 61.

Chapter 7

1. Milbank, *Theology and Social Theory,* 214.

2. Ethan Coen and Joel Coen, *O Brother Where Art Thou?* (London: Faber and Faber Limited, 2000), viii.

3. Quoted in *Robert Bresson,* ed. James Quandt (Toronto: Cinematheque Ontario, 1998), 1.

Chapter 8

1. Michiko Kakutani, "The Art of Humor I," *Paris Review* 136 (1995): 215.
2. Quoted in Bill Flanagan, *U2 at the End of the World* (New York: Delacorte Press, 1995), 171.
3. Stringfellow, *A Keeper of the Word*, 169.
4. Hannah Arendt, *The Human Condition: A Study of the Central Dilemmas Facing Modern Man* (New York: Doubleday Anchor Books, 1959), 214–15.
5. O'Donovan, *The Desire of the Nations*, 268.
6. Milbank, *Theology and Social Theory*, 228.
7. O'Donovan, *The Desire of the Nations*, 109.
8. John Milbank, *The Word Made Strange* (Malden, Mass.: Blackwell, 1997), 228.
9. O'Donovan, *The Desire of the Nations*, 175.
10. O'Connor, *The Habit of Being*, 280.